How to Be Eternally Blessed

by
Richard Poulin

authorHOUSE®

AuthorHouse™
1663 Liberty Drive, Suite 200
Bloomington, IN 47403
www.authorhouse.com
Phone: 1-800-839-8640

© *2008 Richard Poulin. All rights reserved.*

No part of this book may be reproduced, stored in a retrieval system, or transmitted by any means without the written permission of the author.

First published by AuthorHouse 12/19/2008

ISBN: 978-1-4389-2921-7 (sc)

Printed in the United States of America
Bloomington, Indiana

This book is printed on acid-free paper.

Scriptures taken from the HOLY BIBLE, NEW INTERNATIONAL VERSION. Copyright c 1973,1978,1984 by International Bible Society. Used by permission of Zondervan Publishing House. All rights reserved.

TABLE OF CONTENTS

Preface   **vii**

Section I—His Knowledge to Feed On

Chapter 1	Knowing the Truth	3
Chapter 2	Grasping Hold of the Truth	7
Chapter 3	Is It Well With Your Soul?	11
Chapter 4	Benefiting From Our Past	14
Chapter 5	Benefits of Loving His Word	18
Chapter 6	Blessings Of Being Selfless	21
Chapter 7	You Are Highly Valued	24
Chapter 8	Power of Thanksgiving	28
Chapter 9	Digging Deep and Finding Real Treasures	32

Section II—Victorious Living Through Christ Jesus

Chapter 10	Knowing the Enemy	37
Chapter 11	Satan's Guilt Trip	42
Chapter 12	Bondage of Traditions	47
Chapter 13	Do We Believe in Man or God?	50
Chapter 14	Hating What God Hates	53
Chapter 15	Being Stubborn For Jesus	57
Chapter 16	Declaring War on the Real Enemy	60

Section III—Nourishment For Your Soul

Chapter 17	Heart of the Matter	67
Chapter 18	Watching What We Say	69
Chapter 19	Godly Sorrow Vs. Worldly Sorrow	74
Chapter 20	Reaping What You Sow	**77**

Section IV—Blessings To Be Children Of The Light

Chapter 21	Worshipping the Lord	85
Chapter 22	Attributes Of God—Part I	88
Chapter 23	Attributes of God—Part II	92
Chapter 24	Who Will Be the Greatest in His Kingdom?	95
Chapter 25	Receiving His Glorious and Eternal Rewards	98

PREFACE

I believe these chapters will ultimately help you to benefit the most from God's word. The purpose of writing this book is to help Christians develop a deeper understanding of God's word in your life and to be able to understand "how to" get the most value out of His word. Quite frankly, although I know many Christians who mean well, I don't believe they understand the full impact of His word and the consequences of not embracing His word to the extent that I know many should come to know. That is why God instructs us in Proverbs 3:13, "Blessed is the man who finds wisdom, the man who gains understanding." Deeper revelation and knowledge will come into effect when a person understands a concept rather than just knows about it. Therefore, I'm excited and confident that this book will allow you to gain greater insight, knowledge of God's word, and the blessings of gaining understanding in greater detail.

The first section identifies the simplicity of coming to know the deeper truths of God's word, and how to benefit the most so that the power of His word becomes most effective in your life. The second section helps us identify who our real enemy is and to understand who we are in Christ and the authority God has given us. The reason why we need to know about our spiritual enemy is because Christ Himself reveals many times who our enemy is, and his tactics; so that we are not unaware of his schemes. If God didn't want us to know about our enemy (the devil), why would God have mentioned him so many times in scripture? The following section emphasizes our concerted need to feed on the encouragement of His word in order to live the abundant life that Jesus said He came to give us

(John 10:10). This section also deals with the consequences that the devil and his angels can have on a Christian's life when we fail to live in the fullness of God's word, which is His will for us.

The last section discusses the blessings of receiving His word and the positive impact we can have on many people's lives when we choose to live His way. God has proven in His word that He is willing to do more for us than we could ever ask or think (Eph. 3:20). This tells me that we often fail to receive more of God's blessings for us because we take His word lightly, limit His power and love for us, and fail to receive His grace and mercy that He wants to pour out into our lives. We may also fail to see the vitality of the power, the importance and impact that His word can have on our lives. The devil often robs Christians from living the abundant life that Jesus came to offer each of us (3 John: 2; John 10:10). Many people do not believe in living the prosperous life, and they don't understand that the prosperous life is much more than simply money. Jesus mentions many times that He desires that we live the abundant life, and when we turn our backs on that, that is where many Christians are being robbed by our enemy, the devil who comes to rob, kill and destroy (John 10:10a).

You will notice that I always capitalize the words that are directed to Christ and that I purposely do not capitalize the name belonging to the devil, even though it may be at the beginning of a sentence to always remind us that he is a defeated foe in our lives to us who know how to rightfully handle the Truth (Word of God; Jesus) found in 2 Tim. 3:15, 16. You may also notice that I may have duplicated phrases and scriptures just as the Bible often does. This is simply to illustrate the importance of the message to reach the heart and be of utmost blessing to the reader. Therefore, I encourage you to benefit in every way of life by praying, asking, and believing God to reveal the fullness of His good and perfect will for you. Remember, it's up to us how much we are willing to allow God's Spirit to work within each of our lives. God bless you with His word as you allow His precious Holy Spirit to direct you.

SECTION I

His Knowledge to Feed On

Chapter 1

KNOWING THE TRUTH

Today, there are many faiths and denominations divided in their theology about who God is and the truth about Christianity in general. Why is it that so many Christian and different denominations are divided when it comes to knowing what is the truth about doctrine? God never intended us to create a number of denominations. His established church (the people) are intended to be universal as one body with Christ Himself as the head. When we replace Christ with a person to be the head of the church and we follow the doctrine of man and its denomination, division takes place. Only Christ himself is perfect and His ways are just! We need to put our hope in God instead of man because man often becomes unstable in his ways. Only Christ is established in truth because He is truth (John 14:6). If every man followed Christ by the leading of His Holy Spirit, there would never be any division because the Holy Spirit guides us into all truth (John 16:13). When the Spirit guides us into all truth, it is the straight and narrow path that never leads anyone astray. Truth doesn't lead people down various different paths. Truth is established by following one path. People fail to come to know the truth because they fail to do the thing that is so simple—to ask. You have not, because you ask not (James 4:2). Seems pretty simple to me! When you ask and do not receive, you ask with the wrong motives to fulfill the lust of your flesh (James 4:3) along with having impure motives, which ultimately benefits you rather than seeking to bless others. Therefore, there are several reasons why people simply do not receive when they ask. One reason is that they are not humbled with the expectation of receiving from God. Many Christians do not receive His truth because they are already set in their opinions, and they think that they are already established in their hearts. They are not open to ask and receive a revelation of a deeper truth, which the Holy Spirit is able and willing to impart.

Pride is one of the devastating mindsets that blinds people from receiving a deeper knowledge and love for God. God says in His word, "A fool has more hope than someone who is wise in their own eyes" (Proverbs 26:12). God opposes the proud, but gives grace and unmerited favor to the humble (James 4:6). In other words, it's not the intelligent who have the knowledge about the truth, but it is those who have a heart after God, who desire to seek to know Him, and desire a deeper relationship with Him.

People may never receive because they ask as though they are testing God to see if He is true to His promises. One of the very temptations Jesus overcame was to inform the devil of the Word, "For it is written, do not put the Lord your God to the test" (Matt. 4:7). What is hidden in the heart of man is open to God who sees. Don't kid yourself; God knows the condition of your heart and the intentions of your motives!

Therefore, when we ask of God, there are a couple of things we need to do. When we ask, we need to do our part and seek by studying His word. Study the Word to show yourself approved by God so that you are able to handle the word of truth (2 Tim. 2:15). A person doesn't find gold simply by asking. They need to know where to look and do some digging. Secondly, when we ask and seek to receive His knowledge, wisdom and instructions, we need to have a humble heart with the expectation that He will definitely answer our prayers and not lead us astray. In Matt. 7:9-11, it mentions that if you ask for bread, will He give you a stone? If you ask for fish, will He give you a snake? The answer is obviously NO. It goes on to say, if you who are evil know how to give good gifts to your children, how much more will your Heavenly Father give good gifts to those who ask Him? Therefore, if you want to know the absolute truth about any issue/doctrine, ask, seek and be expecting that God will graciously reveal the truth to you. Why would God lead anyone astray? Is it God's will that we remain deceived? Is it God's will that we become divided? Does God not want to reveal His truth to all? Then why is it that very few people know the deeper truth? Otherwise, there would be far less division amongst the churches if it were so. God clearly says that He is not pleased when we are divided with doctrine, which causes only division and strife (1 Cor. 11:17, 18). If God didn't want us to know His absolute truth, why would He have gone through the trouble to leave His throne of glory with God the Father to reveal the written word by His flesh (John 1:1,14) and humble Himself, live the life as a humble servant, and willingly go to the extent of dying the shameful death on the cross? Seems like He would have done this all for nothing if He had not wanted us to know about Himself (the truth)! He warns His people in Hosea 4:6 that, "My people are destroyed from lack of knowledge, because you have rejected knowledge."

When I became a new Christian, I was caught up between divided issues of different doctrines, and I felt like I was being pulled in many directions with different interpretations of doctrine. I eventually went to a solitary place and spent quality time praying to God and seeking His guidance. I expected Him to lead me and guide me to the many answers I was looking for. With a humble heart and the expectation of receiving from Him, He graciously blessed me with answers to my many questions with an inner assurance and peace of what I had come to believe. However, I had to spend time in prayer and studying His word. I also prayed that if there was any subtle error that I was believing in, that He would help me to reject anything that was not the absolute truth of His word.

A gentleman and I were having a disagreement about an issue. I mentioned to him that we should pray about this. He emphatically said "NO" this is the way! Needless to say, I ended that discussion by refusing to listen to such ungodly counsel. In other words, we are encouraged to be gentle in our teaching, but we need to encourage each other to seek the One who is able and willing to lead us into all truth by prayer, before arguing and quarrelling sets in (2 Tim. 2:23,24). I have never known anyone who could argue someone else into knowing the truth or believing any certain doctrine. That is why God's Spirit, who gently leads us to all truth is able to be the most effective way in understanding the truth. It's only knowing the truth and living the truth that you will be set free (John 8:32). Who in their right mind doesn't want to be set free?

Therefore, if you want to know the truth, ask (in prayer), seek (through studying His word) and humble your heart before Him with the expectation of receiving a deeper knowledge of His word and His love by His Spirit. He promises to those who hunger and thirst for righteousness, that they are the ones who shall be filled (Matt. 5:6). When He fills us, we are filled with the knowledge of His word, which frees us from the bondage of doubts and fears, and liberally imparts to us His wisdom, understanding, peace, joy and health (physically, mentally, emotionally and spiritually). He longs to fill each of us with these blessings if we would only be willing to open our heart to Him and believe that He is more than willing and able, and learn to receive His abundant grace to us, if we would only entrust Him and commit every situation unto Him.

"Trust in the Lord with all your heart and lean not on your own understanding; in all your ways acknowledge Him, and He will make your paths straight" (Prov. 3:5,6).

Chapter 2

GRASPING HOLD OF THE TRUTH

It's interesting that Jesus often spoke, and explained His teachings with a physical metaphor to teach us a Biblical understanding of a spiritual truth. One clear example was when the Apostle Paul wrote how we are a spiritual body and he compared it to a physical body, so we could understand how we need each other and must rely on each other. We only work effectively when we are joined together in unity and like-mindedness, praying one for another, encouraging one another, and maintaining fellowship one with another. When we detach ourselves from having fellowship, it's like detaching a part of a physical body, which would be a bad thing! Comparatively, when I was reading through various articles in a Christian magazine, I came across an illustration that utilizes the same principles to get the most of God's word for our benefit. A diagram of a hand is holding the Bible, with four fingers on top of the Bible and the thumb holding it up from underneath. Now, picture that each finger represents a word of an approach to living and working with the Word of God. This is a concept of a most effective method of gaining knowledge and understanding of the scriptures and being able to retain this knowledge. To benefit and impart the knowledge of His truth to others, it is imperative that we develop an effective method to gain more knowledge and wisdom by retaining this revelation in our hearts. Once you understand a concept and it finally gets into your heart because you believe, you can retain this knowledge and impart a vital truth to others as you help teach and instruct others.

This illustration starts with the smallest finger, which had written on it, "Hear." In Rom. 10:17, it tells us how we can build our faith by taking time to hearing and hearing the word of God. A good way of doing this is to read several scriptures audibly to yourself, especially when God is talking about the blessed promises He has in store for you. He talks about His love and protection for you, as it's indicated in Psalm 91; a classic example. I would ask you at this time to go to this passage and begin reading this out loud to yourself because if we need to hear the word to build our faith, then we should apply this principle to speak it audibly to ourselves in order to hear and build our faith. We also need to personalize it. So again, when you read Psalm 91 over again, simply insert your name as though God is speaking directly to you. Every time I have read a passage like this audibly to myself, the effects of the power of His word really touched my heart in a most profound way. The next finger represents "Read." It assures us of His blessedness by reading His word which is a lamp unto our feet and a light unto our path (Psalm 119:105) that directs us to His blessed kingdom. To get the most out of reading, we need to visualize ourselves by being in that particular situation and being honest with ourselves about how we would react to a specific situation. As an example, although we can be critical of Peter for losing faith after briefly walking on the water to Jesus, we need to see if we first would even have dared to get out of the boat to walk on the water to meet Jesus. When we do, it will tell us a lot about ourselves and how much we will get from reading the Word. There are many other illustrations you can use also.

As we move to the middle finger, we have the word, "Study." In Acts 17:11, the Bereans were more noble in character because they received the message with great eagerness, and they examined the scriptures to see the truth, which is able to make you wise for salvation through faith in Christ Jesus (2 Tim. 3:15). Studying to show thyself approved by God, a workman who doesn't need to be ashamed and who correctly handles the Word of truth (2 Tim. 2:15). To help us in our study, rather than just simply memorizing the scriptures word for word, we must retain His word so that we can relate an experience to a previous situation or encounter. Again, what has helped me when studying His word is not to generalize it so much when you fail to personalize it. This lets you know that God is personally interested in you because God wants to have a personal relationship with you in the first place. God is more interested when we desire to have a personal relationship with Him rather than just having knowledge about Him. When you simply have knowledge, but have no relationship to love Him, it means absolutely nothing to Him and we miss out on His blessings and favor upon us entirely.

The next finger along the hand represents, "Memorize." Psalm 119:9-11 shows that by memorizing scripture, it keeps our way pure and we are then able to hide it in our hearts so that we will not sin against God. In addition, when I attempt to memorize sentences or definitions, I go over the concept in my mind and translate it into my own words so I can understand the concept in what is being said. I found that when I was taking a human resource management course, I had a lot of terms in the glossary section I had to know. I learned something valuable when I came to someone and asked him how he got to know so much, and he mentioned to me that he recites what he reads and simply thinks about it for a minute. Then he attempts to put it into his own words. I later realized that it was a clear, simple, and practical way of inheriting this knowledge.

Last, but not least, the thumb, which holds the Bible from underneath represents, "Meditate." By meditating on all that you have heard, read, studied, and memorized, it helps you to gain a greater overall understanding of what God is saying. The more you meditate, the more you will realize that God somehow reveals a deeper revelation to you and you will grasp a greater understanding of His word. Another example is when I took several college courses and a university course. I knew bits and pieces of ways to do accounting in different segments, but it seemed very difficult overall. Once I had applied all my studying, memorizing, learning and reading by meditating and giving thought to all of this, it was only then that the whole concept of financial and managerial accounting became much easier. When we put this physical dimension in a spiritual perspective, we can ask ourselves that if we lack in any of these, it is like severing a finger. In other words, if we do not read, but do the others, it's like cutting off a finger, which means the hand doesn't remain as strong. More so, if you lack in two of the five areas, you cannot expect the hand to be as useful with three fingers as it would be with all the fingers. Therefore, when you put all of these concepts to use, but don't meditate on what you have read, heard, memorized or studied, the thumb which holds the Bible in place drops right out of your hand. Then it's like you have forgotten the important aspect of what you read, studied, heard or memorized. So by applying all these five principles (hearing reading, studying, memorizing and meditating), you will have a good grasp of living and working with the Word of God, which would be most beneficial to you spiritually and in all dimensions of living your life before God. This indicates that this is a practical physical metaphor which will allow us to gain a clearer understanding of how to spiritually benefit in all aspects of our lives.

Additionally, when we read scripture and meditate on His word, it is important that we have the mindset of looking at what we read and ask God; "how do we apply or how does this apply to our lives today"? For instance, when we read about Jonah, we should see it as a principle which we should learn from in our everyday lives, rather than just knowing about this event as some history lesson. The fact that we should learn the error of Jonah's choice of disobeying God, when we need to see this for ourselves. Every story we read, whether it's about Adam, Noah, Abraham or many other characters in the Bible, we need to see how we are to appropriate it to our lives today and learn from these and many other past events God talks about. Just knowing about these events and not applying it to our everyday lives is just gaining head knowledge, having no eternal value.

Finally, it is okay to question God when you want to understand something from His word. It's important to understand that you must have the assurance and expectation that He will answer and give us the truth. When you read Heb. 4:16, He admonishes us to come boldly to His throne of grace so we can receive His grace and mercy in our time of need. However, the term boldly means to come to Him with confidence and not arrogantly.

"But his delight is in the law of the Lord, and on his law he meditates day and night. He is like a tree planted by streams of water which yields its fruit in season and whose leaf doesn't wither. Whatever he does prospers" (Psalm 1:2, 3).

Chapter 3

Is It Well With Your Soul?

When we pray, we often pray for healing of relationships, financial needs, employment, physical healings and many other requests. God is interested in every one of our concerns. However, He is most interested in the well-being of our soul first and foremost. In 3 John: 2, God does say that it is His will that we prosper in all things and walk in divine health, just as our soul prospers. However, this means we must first examine our very soul before we should prosper. When we are admonished to examine our soul, this means we need to examine our motives, our desires, and our ambitions to see whether God would be pleased or not. Do we have more concern for our own well-being more than the benefit of others? Is it well with our soul? What if we do get an answer to prayer for a physical healing, financial blessings, or employment, etc., while it may not be well with our own soul? What good would it do us in the long run? What good would it be if you gained the whole world and lose your soul? When we ask for prayer, we need to examine ourselves to see if there is any place within our soul which needs to be healed. For instance, do we need to forgive others who have trespassed against us? Do we love serving ourselves more than others? How is our relationship with the One who died on the cross for us? Our relationship with God goes hand in hand with the kind of relationship we have with each other. Do I remain covetous and not satisfied? These are just some of the questions you may ask yourself along with many other possible questions. God is truly interested in all we do. He is interested in us so much that He knows our rising up and our sitting down and perceives my thoughts from afar (Psalm 139:2). If you are struggling with unanswered prayers, ask our merciful God to help you take an inventory of what you need to deal with and He will help you. The measure of your asking, believing and receiving His help is the measure He will offer to you. "You have not because you ask not. When you ask, you do not receive because you ask with wrong motives that you may indulge in your pleasures" (James 4:2,3). So when we ask for prayer, are we right with God, first of all? Do we harbor jealousy, envy, or bitterness towards anyone? Do we show contempt towards anyone? A lot of Christians think they can love God and justify harboring bitterness, anger and un-forgiveness to another. Unfortunately for them, they are very much deceived, not knowing that when we love the least of any brethren, we love the Lord to the same measure (read Matt. 25:40). Many of them will stand and sing to the Lord with open arms, but they will gossip and backbite one another as soon as they leave the worship service. Sadly, this is the case and it's one of many reasons why God doesn't move on their behalf. Psalm 66:18 tells us that "if I had cherished sin in my heart, the Lord would not have listened." Also, when we ask for prayer, do we have the intention of giving God the glory and sharing the blessings we receive with others for their benefit? We need to see the positive spiritual impact for every prayer request we ask, so in the end, it will first and foremost be well with our soul, and that our soul will prosper, having His inexpressible joy and full of glory, gladness of heart and the peace which surpasses all understanding. God is first and foremost interested in the well-being of our soul because He knows that the rewards in heaven far exceed any rewards anyone could receive here on earth. That is why He encourages us to set our affections on things above, and not on things of this world (Col. 3:2). In our quest to ask others to pray for us, we need to be determined in our hearts to be strong in the Lord and the power of His might. We need to strengthen our faith in Him, love for Him, love for others and invite His Spirit to grow in us and help us develop a Christ-like character more and more. We miss the point when we pray different prayers for ourselves when we fail to do what He would have us do the most, and that is by asking God to help us become more like Christ. When we love Him, value His word and His help for us, He will give us the grace and strength to be strong in the Lord and do what we would otherwise fail to be able to do in our own strength. Therefore, it is important to be encouraged and ask God to help you examine your soul. When you yield to His loving grace, He will indeed help you and guide you along the best path, which He has planned for your life (Jer. 29:11). When you ask, do it with a humble heart and with the right spirit within you. God will never despise a broken spirit or a contrite heart (Psalm 51:17). He is acquainted with our grief because He has endured many griefs and sorrows, yet was without sin. Since He endured and is acquainted with many griefs and sorrows, He is willing and able to help us in every adverse situation. God is so merciful because His mercy triumphs over judgment (James 2:13). I know this will encourage you in the Lord as it has for myself when you meditate on these principles.

Chapter 4

Benefiting From Our Past

Have you ever noticed that Christ didn't simply choose the most learned, and well-educated men in His time to be His appointed followers? On the contrary, He chose uneducated men who would change the direction of this world of Christianity. If we want to receive more of Christ, we must have that desire and thirst for more of Him. In Matt. 5:6, which is part of the Beatitudes, He says, "He who hungers and thirsts for righteousness shall be filled." It's not simply by being scholarly that we will come to the knowledge of God and His word. I personally am grateful for that!! On the contrary, in 1 Cor. 1:20-25, it tells us that the scholarly who are worldly wise are shamed by those whose heart is hungry for Him. Notice that in Matt. 18:1-4, that anyone will not inherit the Kingdom of God unless he becomes as a child. This means you need to not have the mind of a child, but a heart of a child. Jesus tells His disciples that a person who humbles himself like a child, will be called the greatest in the Kingdom of God. Often times, we do not understand the Word, even though when we read it when it should be very plain to everyone who can read. In Matt. 13:14-15, Jesus describes people who do not understand because of the hardness of their hearts, and it has nothing to do with their intellectual abilities to comprehend. The parable of the sower is a prime example of how some people can be blessed of God by receiving the Word with a good and humble heart who are able to bear much fruit. Or, they can choose to harden their hearts and allow the devil to steal God's very Word, which is the only source that delivers us from bondage; living the life of prosperity (in every arena of our lives), receiving healings and blessings in abundance. As many are well educated and many are mentally challenged, if God were to operate as the world does, the mentally challenged would certainly have a great disadvantage of ever coming to the knowledge of Christ. I can tell you definitely that much of the mentally challenged people I have met would put us to shame when it comes to knowing about God and living the life these people live out each day. Many of us can thank the Lord for not operating the way this world does! However, since that is not the case, everyone has the same advantage because each of us has an equal opportunity to choose. Not one person is at any disadvantage of receiving the riches of God's wisdom and knowledge when it comes to their level of intellect, but a person is at a distinct disadvantage when their hearts are hardened with doubt and unbelief of God's very own Word. That is why Jesus indicates in His word that people are already condemned because they do not believe Him in what He says about who He is (John 3:18). I encourage you not to allow the devil to deceive you by harboring a hardened heart of doubt, unbelief or from past adverse experiences which will only rob you of being blessed. You are the only one who has the ability to allow God to soften your heart and use your past experiences, and to be most useful as a blessed servant used for His glory and be a blessing to others. From my adverse experiences of wandering through deep valleys, it was through those dark periods of my life, from which God was able to turn me around and use me for the purpose of helping and encouraging one another while being a vessel of honor and effectively giving Him glory. With the trials I faced, it was during those times that I decided not to put my hopes and desires for worldly gain, which would have meant that I would have forsaken the greater rewards I now look forward to inheriting in the eternal kingdom in heaven. Therefore, I encourage you to allow God to use your past, whether favorable or traumatic, and ask Him to use it to benefit others and for His glory. When a person has endured many negative situations, he or she has the compassion of Christ when other people are going through a similar crisis. They are the ones whom God especially can use to comfort those who have been comforted in the past. When you use your past experience to bless others, you can be assured that you will be most blessed with joy, peace and satisfaction. Additionally, you will receive His eternal reward. If you allow the devil to keep your heart hardened, only you will fail to receive God's blessings. You alone will suffer the consequences and be defeated. A good example is when Joseph's brothers turned against him, and he was beaten and thrown into a pit where they abandoned him. Then after being taken to Egypt, he was put into prison because of being wrongfully accused by Potipher's wife of having an affair with her when we know he was completely innocent (Gen. 39:6-20). Joseph was able to go from the prison cell to the palace and became the second most powerful ruler in Egypt to Pharaoh himself because he remained faithful to God by fully trusting and believing that He would work things out for Him. It may seem very difficult when injustice against us occurs, but we have the assurance that God will never allow us to go through any trial that we cannot bear and know that each person reaps exactly what they sow. I believe when God puts us through the greatest tests and we endure them, it becomes the greatest avenue for us so we can be highly valued for His use. The best flavored tea is made when the water comes to a full boil; the best china is made went it goes through the flaming fires. Roses give off the best perfumed scent when they are trampled on. With these illustrations, we can identify that the ones who are often used effectively for God's purposes are the ones who went through many trials. "Praise God and Father of our Lord Jesus Christ, the Father of compassion and the God of all comfort, who comforts us in all our troubles, so that we can comfort those in any trouble with the comfort we ourselves have received from God," NIV (2 Cor. 1:3,4). If I had never needed to be comforted by God from my past and the trials I endured, I would never have known how to comfort others in similar troubles they were facing. Again, it's important to note that people who are going through trials are able to respect those who have gone through similar trials because they're the ones who understand similar painful experiences certain people may be going through. Most people become upset and frustrated when other people try to give advice, but they don't understand their pain because they may not have gone through a similar experience. Job himself was frustrated with his friends because they spoke as though they had all the answers and the solution to his problem, when all along, Job wanted his friends to help carry his burdens through understanding, and by having a listening ear, a listening heart, and receiving encouragement by interceding on his behalf through prayer. God Himself displayed His great displeasure to Job's friends because they lacked a compassionate and understanding heart. They failed to listen; rather, they lectured.

It's a blessing knowing that no matter how bad our past may have been, God can turn our adversities around to help someone. I have seen the most effective witness of any person who can touch lives of many people in profound ways. They are the ones who have been through adversities and are now testifying how God dramatically changed their lives for the better. If they had continued to wallow in their past, like the devil likes to keep people in bondage to, those people would have never known how the lives of many others would have been changed for the better had they not used God's help to use their past to bless others in their time of need. We will not lose our reward, which God graciously awaits to give us when we are faithful to Him, to His cause, and to know we have eased the burdens of the oppressed, while being a blessing to them in their time of need. When we help one another and ease their burdens, we see the purpose of this which bridges the gap of separation and unifies us with greater expressions of joy, peace, and gladness that builds healthy relationships.

Chapter 5

Benefits of Loving His Word

I was inspired by David's message in Psalm 119:11-19. When we see that His word is a true inspiration of His love, we know that we serve a God who is infinite and perfect in Love, and is always giving. God instructs his children to be still and know that, "I am God" (Psalm 46:10; Job 37:14). We should take our time in quiet meditation to realize that His word gives us the very instructions to direct us in living the life of being so blessed with His divine presence. We need to understand that the instruction of His word is the way which we will receive the utmost blessings to inherit, not only for this world, but in the realm of eternity that has no end. When we realize this, we should be inspired to live by His word and come to love His word that Jesus Himself has fulfilled perfectly. When we see what Jesus has done for us, providing the power of His Spirit to lovingly instruct us, guide us, and that He has prepared a glorious eternal place for us, we should ultimately want to love His word and delight in His laws as mentioned throughout the Psalms. When we choose to live by the vain philosophies of man and what this world offers, it would only delight the hearers who want to hear instruction that satisfies the soul which benefits us for only a mere moment in time. As it says in Psalm 119:96, only God's laws are boundless. It's God's laws and instructions that bring everlasting joy and peace to those who hear not only what they want to, but gladly receive the word they know they need to hear. When we read John 6:60-69, this is the time when Jesus had many disciples other than the twelve, who had left Him because they could not accept His teaching. Notice in particular verses 66-69 where Jesus asked the twelve if they also wanted to leave. I like the response Peter gave when he replied, "Lord, to whom shall we go? You alone have the Words to eternal life. We believe and know that You are the Holy One of God." Peter knew the rich value of His divine word, whereby anything else that didn't speak the same language had no value of eternal life whatsoever. We have to understand that it is only God's ways that direct us in how to have eternal life and eternal blessings of peace, joy and gladness. This is why His word should be greater than all the treasures of this world. Having all the wealth will only bring temporal happiness, but only God's word gives us what is priceless—inner peace, joy inexpressible and full of glory, gladness of heart, and peace which surpasses all understanding. The rewards and benefits of allowing God's word to have authority in our lives has an eternal inheritance unsurpassed by what this world could ever offer. The richest man in this world can never compare to what God offers us for free. It's awesome to think of the great price Jesus paid for us, and that we should receive the greatest miracle of all—salvation, when we invite Jesus to be our personal Lord and Saviour. As His word is divinely inspired by God (2 Tim. 3:16), it should cause us to have a divine love for His word, His laws, and His instructions for our lives. This will help us each time we open our Bibles to receive His word with delight in our hearts. In the parable of the Seed and the Sower, the word will have no effect if our hearts are hard, the cares of this world (infesting weeds) are choking the blessings of His word, or if we do not develop roots and become established in His word, and in our love for Him. When our hearts are right before Him, His word will have a blessed effect on our lives. We will bear much fruit as we are called to do. Our hearts can be right before Him as we confess our faults, confess our need of Him, and believe that we will receive the very best from Him. We must know that He loves us and cares for us more than anyone else could ever do. When we see the truth of His divine and unconditional love for us when we precede to read His word, I believe His word will take on a greater meaning. We will know that the richest treasures of all are truly found in His word. We may not like His instructions at times, nor entirely agree with them, but it is what is ultimately the best for us in the boundless realm of eternity. Any other instruction that violates His word is compared to building our houses (lives) upon sinking sand which will never be stable. We end up living in a false sense of hope that will never satisfy. People who take God's word lightly or do not value His word will always end up living with regret. The laws of this world confine us to be under legalism, whereas God's laws liberate us from all bondage of sin. Sin is what keeps man captive by being a slave to the one who wants to rob, steal and destroy our lives. His word is what frees us from this bondage. The amount of our freedom is in relation to how much we acknowledge our need of God, know the importance of His word, and love His word. Knowing this in your heart should cause you to love His laws and instruction for you each time you read and study His word.

Chapter 6

Blessings Of Being Selfless

Have you ever noticed a person who is selfish and/or arrogant to ever be filled with joy and inner peace? Strangely enough, according to the world's expectations, I have yet to meet a happy, joyful and peaceable person who is stingy and self-centered. It's ironic that many people think that acquiring material wealth, monetary value, and serving "self" will bring true joy and peace. Tragically, many people have sought to take a life of a living soul for their personal gain and self-glorification only for a very brief moment in time at the expense of their soul in the eternal realm of hell, fire and darkness where no hope of rest or peace will ever be experienced. Even for all the wealth, worldly fame, and glory, this world could ever give, it will never compare when you are living according to God's instructions, which is the only means that gives you the priceless intangible benefits of having peace within, gladness within your heart, and the joy that comes by knowing Jesus personally. Jesus compared one soul far more valuable than all the riches of this world. What good would it be that one would gain the whole world and lose its soul (Matt. 16:26)? I see the most precious people in this world are the ones who selflessly give unto others. The joy and peace fills their hearts and you can clearly see the radiance of God's glory when they serve others rather than themselves. People who continue to be selfish by having that "me, myself and I" attitude are never able to inherit the priceless gifts of having joy, peace, and freedom from all fears.

I learned even as a young boy that I found more joy in giving than receiving, especially at Christmas time. There is something valuable that nothing in the world can compare to when you share your "self" with others. It may be money, clothing, food, or just your time in fellowship and prayer. I have found that a lot of elderly, in particular, treasure the time you spend with them. They realize that when someone invests their time with them, it is something that no tangible gift could ever compare to.

Jesus tells us that our religion, or our good works are not indicated by becoming self-glorified by living a good life, but rather, to clothe the naked, feed the hungry, visit the sick and those in prison (Read Isaiah. 58:7 and James 1:27). When we do these things, we do it unto Him. He tells us that when He was naked, sick, or in prison, He said that it didn't matter whether we did it unto Him or not. But, the important aspect is to realize that what we do unto others, we ultimately treat our Lord in the same manner (Matt. 25:36-40). We don't have to give a big charitable donation for God to be pleased with us. Jesus was more pleased with the poor widow giving two mites than the rich people giving from their abundance. Therefore, it's not the amount of your giving or the size of your ministry God is pleased with. He is most pleased when we have a heart after Him by living with a desire to serve Him as we serve one another. As you read about the parable of the talents, you will notice the joy of the two servants who used their talents that God gave them by benefiting others. However, notice how despondent the one servant was by simply hiding his talent and never using it? This type of servant is only interested in serving the "self" and not using it for the benefit of others. He was more interested in his reputation and fear of not trusting in God's provision that He promises to give us (read Matt. 25:14-30).

Similarly, the richest man in the world will never have any hope or peace simply by relying on his riches. When you share the most precious commodity—yourself—in service to others and in the admonition of the Lord, it is a value unsurpassed that money could never afford. When you do share a part of you, our most precious Lord fills you with the priceless gift of His peace that surpasses all understanding, with joy inexpressible and full of glory and gladness of heart. That is why it is truly more blessed to give than to receive (Acts 20:35). The world still has yet to prove it otherwise. It's no coincidence that I witness time and time again, that the people in the same degree who are more selfish are the ones who remain more angry and bitter about issues of their own lives in general.

It's also true when I consider others in their time of grief, that somehow, the trials that I have gone through during that same time seem as nothing when I decide to show them kindness and compassion in their time of need, rather than to wallow in self-pity. There is nothing like the joy of giving one's selfless deeds unto others. When you offer yourself to benefit others, you're giving them the best that no material gifts this world could ever compare to. God promises to us, that we will be rewarded when our deeds blesses others and gives God the glory. This is a perfect illustration about our responsibility of being imitators of Christ (Eph. 5:1) because Christ himself was the perfect example of living a self-less life.

Chapter 7

YOU ARE HIGHLY VALUED

One of the devastating effects the devil is having upon the Church (Believers in Christ) today is that many remain in their comfort zone. Many Christians today simply go to a worship service each week to hear the word of God, but they don't go into their neighborhood to witness, encourage the broken-hearted, serve others, or be mindful towards one another in prayer for their needs. A lot of Christians think that this is the job of a pastor, the elders, or the evangelist. Complacency is one of the devastating tools the devil uses against God's people. Many people often feel like they are vulnerable or inadequate because of their lack of physical abilities, talents, a lack of education, or even intelligence. When they feel like that and believe it, they are believing the lies of the devil. When there are many elderly members in the church, it devastates my soul to hear them say, "I'm too old"!! If that were so, why would God continue to keep them alive? As long as God keeps you alive, you remain useful as a precious tool for Him and for His purpose, because everything He does, has a significant purpose to fulfill His divine plan. His divine plan includes each and every one of us. If we are too old to pray or make intercession, then there's a definite problem with the way they think! I once heard that you become the type of person according to the way you think you are. If we think lowly about ourselves, then we end up living the same way with the expectation of being lowly. This is also a deception of the devil. When we have this mindset, we have false humility. Although we are to be humble (by always confessing our need for God), it is important that we declare how highly valued we are in Him. These are a fraction of the many scriptures that teach us that we are more than conquerors through Him who loves us

(Rom. 8:37); that we are seated in heavenly places with Him (Eph. 2:6); we are the head and not the tail; above and not below (Deut. 28:13). We encourage ourselves with the God's word, not because we ever deserve it, but it indicates the type of His grace and mercy that He so much wants to impart to us and it identifies the truth about who we really are in Christ. If we ever received God's blessings because we deserved it, His grace He desires to give us would not be considered His gift to us in the first place. God's mercy is pardoning the punishment we should have received before we repented, and His grace is the unmerited favor He longs to give us when we don't deserve it. In Eph. 3:20, it indicates that He is willing and able to do exceedingly and abundantly more than what we could ever ask or think. This indicates to me that there are far too many Christians who rob God's blessings for them because they believe in the false humility concept that by being a Christian, we need to remain poor and think lowly about ourselves. This is one of the lies from the pit of hell that indicates that the devil ends up fulfilling his plan to rob, kill and destroy us, whereby Christ came so that we would have life and have it in abundance (John 10:10). Also, many people feel inadequate because they don't take part in the leadership of the church. These people often feel insecure because they think they are of little use. That is another lie of the devil to deceive many people to think this way. Notice what it says in   1 Cor. 12:12-26 when God compares the physical body to the spiritual body of Christ. In verses 23 and 24, it says, "The parts that we think are less honorable, we treat with special honor, and the parts that are un-presentable are treated with special modesty while our presentable parts need no special treatment. God has combined the members of the body and has given greater honor to the parts that lacked it." In the eyes of God, no matter who you are, when you understand the magnificent truth of His love for you, you will know you are highly valuable in His sight. He can use you to bless others and fulfill His plan most effectively if you desire to be used by Him and believe He is able to use you as a valuable member. No matter how talented you are, or how insignificant you may see yourself, all members of the body are vital and necessary to be most effective for His cause, because it is the power of Christ who lives within us that enables us to do His work in the first place. For without Christ, no man can do anything (John 15:5). For God also admonishes people not to rush to be a spiritual leader or a teacher of the Word because of the great responsibility they have, and those who have received much, much will be required of him (Luke 12:48).

As I was meditating about the members of the body, I looked at the many tiny hairs on my arms. If a person were to compare themselves to a tiny piece of hair, they may see themselves as insignificant. However, among many of those tiny hairs, it was those hairs collectively that often prevented my arms from getting a sunburn. In comparison, it is therefore safe to say that when anyone feels insignificant in the body of Christ, rebuke this lie of the devil because you may be called to pray for someone and save them from being harmed because of your faithful prayers. If it weren't for the tiny hairs along the blood vessel called capillaries, the blood would not be able to flow upwards and reach the vital organs in which life itself is sustained and preserved. In other words, what you may think is insignificant is highly valuable for maintaining a spiritually healthy body. Could you imagine if no one wanted to be a janitor or a cleaner, but everyone wanted to be an elder, or someone in authority? It's like having a body with many mouths, and no feet or hands, etc. Without a cleaner, the building itself would become littered with dust-balls, and then debris and sickness would become rampant.

Therefore, God has given them honor in His sight because He has called different people to different areas in ministry to create that perfect body (the Church) for His ultimate glory. Not one type of ministry is greater than another type of ministry if God has called you specifically to do a particular service. If someone is called to be a greeter at the door, and that person tries to become a pastor, when he had not been called to do it, it will never work. God rewards those who are faithful to Him, not simply because of any position they have attained. The elderly, the infants, the mentally challenged, and the physically challenged are equally precious in the sight of God as is the most gifted preacher or talented singer. Each one of those people, including many others, are highly valuable in His sight. It is important to know that each one of us is a unique individual which God has purposefully created, that no one else can do all that we can collectively do. We fail to see the value of our uniqueness when we desire to be like someone else and try to copy someone else. In other words, you are a priceless original copy. I encourage you to be a beautiful copy of who God created you to be and not to be a cheap imitator by trying to be somebody you are not. The only one we are called to imitate is Christ. God has a purpose for each and every one of us. Each of us is able to be most useful for His purpose if we choose to believe it and ask Him. The greatest handicap we have is often believing the lies of the devil who would make us believe that we are living godly by keeping a low self-esteem about ourselves.

We, in ourselves, can do nothing without Christ. Therefore, no matter who you are, the One who lives in you is able to make you most effective and useful to keep the body of Christ spiritually healthy. All we need to do is choose to believe who we are in Christ. We are simply to believe in the One whom the Father has sent (John 6:29). Remember, a small piece of metal may be all it takes to keep a wagon from coming to a sudden crash. You may feel like that insignificant piece of metal, but it is a vital part of the structure of the wagon if it is to operate at all. Therefore, each of you are vital in the sight of God and useful to do His good and perfect will. Just think of what a great price God gave to sacrifice His own Son in order to redeem a soul such as I. When we know this in our hearts, we know we are highly valued by the One who genuinely loves us. He suffered by having carried our burdens, bore our iniquities by being bruised, bore the painful stripes from being whipped in order that we may claim healing. He willingly died the shameful death on the cross where we should have been taking that penalty instead. Therefore, I cannot stress the importance that you personally know in your heart and in your spirit, that Jesus loves you and values you so much, that if you were the only one living in this world, God the Father would have sent His Son to this world and Jesus would have willingly suffered and died the same way in order to redeem your life in order for you to have the same opportunity of having eternal life.

Chapter 8

POWER OF THANKSGIVING

There is a tremendous blessing when one is thankful to God. Many circumstances may cause us not to want to give God thanks. However, as I reflect on my past, it's amazing how severe negative circumstances I have endured, could turn my life around for the better. I'm more blessed today by having gone through the trials and sufferings than if I had never walked through the valley of discouragement. Looking back and knowing this now, I can truly be thankful of the outcome of my character God has molded me. I truly believe that I have become a much better person because of how God has used me to bless others had I not endured hardships. Mind you, like Paul says, I can also say of myself that I have not reached the goal of becoming like Christ, but I'm grateful that I am not like what I used to be.

God has a plan for each of us, and He clearly says in Jeremiah 29:11 that His plan is for us to have bright hope and a bright future, to prosper and not harm you. We can receive healing from God in many ways—physical healing, emotional healing, financial healing, healing from broken relationships, healing of a broken heart, and most of all, spiritual healing. However, when we are thankful to God, we will receive more than just healing. If you take a close look at the story of the ten lepers (Luke 17:11-19), Jesus healed all of them, but only one returned to Jesus to say, "Thank you." Jesus said that one who was thankful, that in addition to his healing, he was made whole!! The other nine who didn't give thanks were simply cleansed, but were not made whole simply because they were thankless. Leprosy is a disease that eats away at the hands and feet, and it often leaves physical scars, deformed faces, hands and feet. The nine who didn't give thanks may have left cleansed, but they still had deformed hands, feet and scarred faces. The one who came back to Jesus to say thanks was made whole, in addition, he was fully restored. The power of giving heartfelt thanks to God goes a long way. When we are truly thankful to God, we receive more from Him than we had otherwise expected. He is most pleased when we give Him thanks in good times and in bad times, because He is refining us, like unto a precious gemstone, that we may be a precious and useful vessel. His plan for us may not take us along the smoothest path, but the rewards of trusting in Him and giving Him heartfelt thanks are far greater in our favor for all eternity, because we receive the very best when we trust in Him. I encourage you, regardless of your situation, to start giving thanks to God. Then just watch Him move supernaturally in your life. Remember, it is the devil's will that we look at our adverse circumstances (present or past) and become discouraged. He will keep you from having the faith to believe God and give Him thanks and praise, who alone loves you more than anyone could ever do. The natural man, who has never invited Jesus to be his Lord and personal savior can only look and see in the natural, but the spiritual man can see with the eyes of faith, what a loving God is doing to mold us and fashion us to be that blessed vessel that He can use (1 Cor. 2:13-16). Since the day we accepted Jesus to be our Lord and savior, we can see the light of His word because in 1 Cor. 2:14, it says, "The man without the Spirit doesn't accept the things that come from the Spirit of God, for they are foolishness to him, and he cannot understand them, because they are spiritually discerned." That is why we cannot become frustrated when we try to explain God's ways to a person who doesn't believe.

When God attempts to refine us for our good, we often compare negative experiences to a lump of unused clay that is getting ready to go on a spinning wheel and the potter Himself slowly molds us and fashions us to be the type of person He can effectively use us to be. Where God sees an end product as a fine porcelain china cup, we, in our humanity, only see the present adversity. We tend to forget that we are in the loving and mighty hand of God who sees the beginning and the end. The most beautiful china had to go through many spinning cycles, forming the piece by changing the shape of our character, going several times through the fire and finally being adorned and ready to be used. In Rom. 4:20-22, God tells us that Abraham became so strong in his faith in God that he was declared a righteous man before God. When we are declared righteous before God, it simply means that we believe what God says who He is and believe the promises He says He will do when we are obedient to Him. However, you will notice that because of this, Abraham gave glory to God. The point of this matter is that when we give glory to God, our praises and thanksgiving unto Him is what brings Him glory and honor. When we fail to give God our deepest thanksgiving, we become disillusioned. Our hearts become calloused and we fail to receive the blessings of having peace, joy, gladness of heart, and living the abundant life God so desires to give us. When we realize from our past adversities which we have made it through with God's help, we are most joyful when we triumph over an adverse situation than had we never gone through any trial in the first place. We would never appreciate the good times if we never go through hardships.

Do you ever notice that when you are thankful, a sense of peace, joy and gladness fills you. The same thing holds true when another person is unthankful. You will notice that bitterness and jealousy fills their inner man, and that person ends up having no peace or joy. When we give God thanks, we are not simply being nice, but the fact that God is truly worthy to be thanked because He continually sustains life, provides abundantly for us and protects us from so many possible immanent dangers that we are not aware of. When we are thankless to God, we fail to see the truth of His loving kindness to us, and we will end up living in remorse, regret and most of all – with no peace.

Therefore, we can believe God is preparing us for the best of what He can do through us. With this mindset, we can always be thankful because we know that He can only effectively use us when we have been tested and tried. When we pass the test by consistently trusting in Him, we will ultimately receive that incorruptible crown that He is eagerly ready to reward us with (1 Cor. 9:24,25). When we know the truth about Him and that He is willing to do more for us than what we could ever ask or comprehend, we can always be thankful because we know the absolute truth about His immeasurable love for each of us. One scripture I really like to remember when I go through trials is Romans 8:18 "I consider that our present sufferings are not worth comparing with the glory that will be revealed in us." As long as we have Jesus as our Lord, we can always rejoice of having this hope He gives us no matter what the circumstances of life here on earth may bring you.

Chapter 9

Digging Deep and Finding Real Treasures

Many times, people would ask me what was preached the other day, or what I had learned in Sunday school class yesterday. Sometimes I would honestly have forgotten and I would feel embarrassed. I had to seriously think to myself how I would effectively benefit to get the most out of God's word, which is vital for living the victorious life. Sometimes when we skim over phrases like just mere words, it doesn't penetrate within the heart. When we want to receive the richest of treasures, we need to dig deeper. The Lord gave me an illustration of two mining companies. It's neat how God continues to use many simple instructions for various individuals in order to teach a vital and profound principle.

Each company had the same number of machines, equipment and laborers. Company A had a one-hundred square mile area to dig, while Company B had a mere five square mile area. Both companies had the same amount of equipment and they completed their digging tasks at the same time. Although Company B had far less of an area, they spent most their time digging deeper. The first company had barely dug under the surface of the soil. Even though Company A had a land mass of twenty times the size, it was Company B that retrieved the riches of the hidden treasures, because they took their time to dig deeper to find where the rich treasures were buried. God was illustrating this in comparison to reading His word. Although many will attempt to read the Bible in a year, the question is how many treasures (knowledge and wisdom) of His word did we actually receive? Did His word have any more impact than before? Sometimes it is better to read one paragraph of God's word in an evening, and then ponder your thoughts over it and receive a revelation, than simply just skimming over several chapters of His word, like letters on a piece of paper. I find that when I get the most from His word, I relate it to a situation where I have experienced or can imagine a similar situation from my past. As you ponder His word by digging deeper, God is able to reveal the rich, deep treasures of His word in a greater way and gives us deeper insight and discernment. As an example, if you were to read Psalm 139:17,18, it mentions His thoughts. How many times would people just skim over this message and read on? But if you stop and ponder about this for a minute, just think of scooping one averaged-sized bucket of sand. If I were to compare my thoughts to the amount of grains of sand in one bucket, I would be excited knowing my thoughts would match that. Now, let's think of all the beaches in your country, in your continent, in the other six continents, in Hawaii and thousands upon thousands of islands throughout the world. Some of the beaches where I have visited are over five miles long, like the some of the biggest ones I've visited in Honolulu and Rio de Janiero. In His word, it says His thoughts exceed the sum of the total amounts of the grains of sand! Do you see the impact that has if we would just stop to consider the words instead of reading to the end of the passage, or the book? This is one of the awesome attributes of the God we serve. It should cause us to fear in reverence to Him! Also, read the last verse of the last chapter in the book of John. All the books combined in all the world could never tell all that God has done. If you were to stop and just think about that, it should be mind boggling to you. When we think of all the thousands upon thousands of large libraries and schools that have tens of thousands of books each, yet billions upon billions of volumes will never match up to what God has done! If you want to get the most out of God's word, ask God to help you dig deeper in His word so that you can find the greatest treasures. Then take the time to reflect on what you have read. When we ponder His word in our hearts longer, we can keep the rich treasures of His word within our hearts, just like Mary did (Luke 2:19). When you really dig deep in God's word as you ponder and meditate what you have read and studied, you will understand that the treasures of His word do actually exceed all the treasures this world could ever offer! Seek and you will find (Matt. 7:7). The treasures of this world, be it gold, silver or any costly stones last only but a brief moment in the time of our eternal existence. However, the treasures of knowing God and having that deep relationship with Him, exceeds our comprehension of the blessings of what lies in the eternal realm of His glory that awaits us because we have our hope set in Christ Jesus himself.

When we don't take the time to dig deep in His word, we lack bearing the fruit of patience which is vital to our growth in Christ. We have also allowed the devil to rob us by not receiving as much of the Word as we could have benefited from, which is what allows us to live the abundant life (John 10:10). When we take the time to study, we realize our destiny hangs onto how we handle His word. Then, we will see the wonderful truth of how rich, awesome, valuable and vital His word is to each of us.

Finally, when we want to retain what we have heard, we need to exercise our minds, just like a body needs to be exercised when we want to get our bodies in shape. By retaining the information we have learned, we need to go over the message in our minds and meditate by using the message and translating it in our own way of thinking in a way we can understand. That's why I believe studying several different translations of the Bible is not such a bad thing; especially when one version can expound on a concept and another version can say the same thing, but allows us to see it in a different perspective. By making use of exercising our minds to recite any preaching that has been taught, it will help us to retain it by being purposeful and giving thought to what we have heard. When we use this principle, we will be able to fully understand the concept in our own mind and be practical in our teaching when we need to share a vital truth to others as we compare it to God's word.

SECTION II

Victorious Living Through Christ Jesus

Chapter 10

Knowing the Enemy

This segment is particularly important because we, as Christians, need to understand that we fight a spiritual warfare, whether we like to admit it or not. To live the life of victory, we have to understand that we have a spiritual enemy, and we must know about him and his ways. A lot of Christians don't think it's important to know about our enemy. However, when a nation is called to go to war, they are able to defeat the enemy when they know about them and their strategies. If God didn't want us to know about satan (our enemy) and the kingdom of darkness, why would God have mentioned him so many times in His word? God talks about the devil, the kingdom of darkness, and hell, more times than He talks about heaven. Although we have the promises of claiming victory through Christ Jesus as promised in His word, God's people do not often experience their lives as living victoriously in Christ. Again, we need to know about our enemy (the devil and his angels) if we expect to have victory over the tactics they use against us. That's why God often talks about our enemy because He wants us to know about him, and how he attacks, so that we will not be caught off guard or sidetracked by his deceptive ways. The Bible makes it quite clear that we will go through trials. He wouldn't tell us that we needed to be fitted with the amour of God if we would never need it in the first place. Although we will fight spiritual battles, we first need to know when we make Jesus our "Commander-in-Chief," we will never be defeated. We become most effective when we submit to Him first, and then resist the devil. He promises that the devil will flee (James 4:7). This also doesn't mean that we will never have any battles to fight in the first place. One of the imminent dangers of many people, including Christians is when we allow the devil to take control of us, by becoming critical towards one another. Jesus gave an important illustration that when we are critical of one another, and when we see a speck in their eye, we lack seeing the biggest problem of all—ourselves (having the plank in our own eyes). The Pharisees, Sadducees and the teachers of the law who saw themselves as "self-righteous" were the ones Jesus was most displeased with. He often mentioned that they would bear the greater condemnation because of their critical attitudes toward those who they felt were not upholding the law. We forget that it was not us who first chosen to serve God, but it was God who first chose us. In other words, we could still be living under the power of sin and be living the most despicable lifestyle like many do, if it weren't for the grace of God to begin with. I'm reminded of the song I sing about Christ who looked beyond my faults and saw my need. The most ruthless men who live today have no idea of the power of the deception in which the god of this world (which satan is depicted as) has blinded them. If they all knew the spiritual realm in which we are blessed, and that has been revealed to us, they, too, would immediately repent and be made right with God in seconds. When we look past the faults of the unbeliever and the evil doers, we see their need and we're able to do what no ungodly person could ever do, and that is to have compassion on our enemies and pray for them as Jesus tells us to. This is part of what having Godly sorrow means as opposed to having worldly sorrow. One will bring forth life and the other will bring forth death, namely worldly sorrow (read 2 Cor. 7:10). Jesus says if we love the lovely, what reward will we get? Are not even the tax collectors doing that? And if you greet only your brothers, what are you doing more than others? Don't the pagans do that? (Matt. 5:46,47) Another danger I see among many Christians is that partiality is rampant. One will esteem more than others while putting down others or treating them with contempt or clearly showing favoritism. Showing partiality according to His word is sin. Some may think that some sins may be taken lightly. However, no sin is to be taken lightly because it cost Jesus by going all the way to the shameful death on the cross. Also, we must deal with temptation and issues the same way—with partiality, because partiality is considered sin (1 Tim. 5:21).

People may not achieve or live up to the standard of our expectations. However, we must remember that if we were to walk in their shoes, maybe we would be better at understanding their needs and we might look past their faults. God has often shown me in my past where when I was critical of someone in a particular area, I ended up doing the same thing, and God had to sharply convict me of that. I encourage you to not be a vessel used and deceived by the devil. Instead of using your time to do the devil's work by criticizing others, and judging others, you need to do what Jesus would do and that is to encourage and pray for others. Sadly, I really believe the devil doesn't have to concern himself with a lot of churches because there is so much gossiping, back-biting and slandering one another that they become vulnerable by doing his dirty work without him having to interfere any longer. We fight effectively when we are united in love with Him, with one another, and when we focus our hearts to do what God instructs each of us to do in the first place. "But encourage one another daily, as long as it is called today, so that none of you may be hardened by sin's deceitfulness" (Heb. 3:13).

One of the other main tactics the devil uses is for Christians to value God's word lightly, whereby we become stagnant and de-sensitized to the leading of His Spirit, who helps and guides us on the right path. When we become sluggish in our walk with God, it's like comparing a pool of stagnant water, which becomes useless and is full of stench. Unless we plant seeds of His love, and purposefully doing good unto others, we also will become stagnant and stunted in our growth. In addition, when we don't strive to remain in a right relationship with God by reading, praying and studying His word, we not only rob ourselves, but we rob others, including our own families because we failed to be prepared to be a blessing by becoming careless. Church members may have had to rely on us for prayer and encouragement which we would be able to provide effectively had we valued our dependency on God, His word, and the help of His Spirit. We deceive ourselves from living the abundant life Jesus wants us to have (John 10:10) when we don't value God's word the way we should. In 1 Thess 5:19, the Word tells us not to quench the Holy Spirit. The NIV version of the Bible puts it this way, "Do not put out the Spirit's fire."

When we become de-sensitized by not valuing His word as we should, we fail to see the importance of unity within the body. It's a value unsurpassed and words cannot express the importance of a body of believers coming together in unity with each another. Jesus explains in Mark 3:24 that a kingdom cannot stand if it is divided. I believe that the trinity of God is perfect in power because God the Father, the Son and the Holy Spirit are equally perfect in unity. If the devil can keep us off track by being divided and keep us blind from the importance of being unified, he continues to be successful in keeping members of the church spiritually weak. Very good illustrations of how we should be united and be wary of the destruction of people who cause divisions is written in 1 Cor. 1:10-17; and 1 Cor. 3:1-15. When we don't purposefully value God's word and realize that it is the very key to eternal life, we have allowed the devil to rob us and many others including the church. We may have failed in being a blessing to others in their time of need had we been sensitive and obedient to His word.

We are most effective in our spiritual battle when we value His word, and when we ask and receive His help of the Holy Spirit. Then, we can effectively stand in the gap one for another in a time where many people often and desperately need Christians to pray and intercede for them. Although we may see the sins of others, we must guard ourselves from becoming critical. In Gen. 9:20-27, we see that Noah had gotten drunk when he drank of the wine from his vineyard. When Ham came in, the Bible mentions that he saw his father's nakedness and he told his other brothers of this incident. The other two did what was right, by looking away from their father's sin (his nakedness) and covering him. The important emphasis is that Ham was cursed by his father because he was compared to gloating over the sin of another person and he gossiped about it, when he should have done what his other two brothers did. Shem and Japheth were blessed, because this illustrates that God blesses those who do not gloat over someone else's sins, but chooses to cover them in prayer instead. This is why the enemy uses and entices people to spread venomous words of gossip and slander, when we should be aware of his deadly schemes and fight the spiritual battles by praying one for another and cease to gossip of the sins others have committed.

Chapter 11

SATAN'S GUILT TRIP

I would like you to notice that I purposely keep the word "satan" in lowercase letters to remind you that we know he is a defeated enemy. One of the things I have often noticed, is that the devil keeps putting a guilt trip on a lot of Christians who feel selfish when they ask for prayer for themselves. There is certainly nothing wrong with asking something for yourself through prayer. Don't allow the devil to make you feel guilty about praying for yourself. Remember, one of the devil's main tasks is to rob you, and he does just when he makes you think this way. When you read John 17, you will notice that before Jesus prays for His disciples and for believers, He prays for Himself first. If this is the example of Jesus, who is holy, pure and righteous, would it not be so for us? He is the most selfless man to ever live, so this in itself would not be selfish of us to do. If you feel selfish about this, it's time for you to rebuke the devil and his lies in the name of Jesus. Eph. 5:1 tells us to be imitators of Christ. In 1 Chron.. 4:9-10, Jabez prays the prayer of blessings for himself. He was asking God that He would be blessed indeed! God granted Jabez his request to extend his territory and that His hand would be upon him and that harm would not come to him and cause him pain. When we ask to be blessed, we should not feel selfish if we ask with the right motive so that it blesses others. How can we be a blessing to others if we ourselves are not first blessed? How can we give in areas we lack? When we ask God to bless us, and to extend our territory in order to bless more people in our lives, this should be our desire. We should not feel ashamed and guilty about it. When Jesus blessed the children and adults, they certainly didn't feel guilty! If it were so, then why would Jesus be pleased to bless so many people?

Why would Jesus be so pleased to heal many people who desired to be healed and prayed over by Him if it is not His perfect will in the first place? Don't let the devil deceive you any longer and make you feel guilty when you pray for yourself. God convicts us so that we may repent of the wrong we have done. He wants us to be cleansed and we are pardoned from all sin. He wants us to turn away from sin, whereas the devil will put the guilt factor on you and keep you feeling condemned. The devil is a deceiver and a liar. He will rob you of any blessing you allow him to.

The devil will try to make you remain guilty because of whatever ungodly deeds you may have done in the past. Sometimes we feel justified to receive God's pardon by continuing to feel guilty or condemned about our past. This is a deceptive and deadly strategy of the devil because he knows if he can get us to think this way, it robs us of developing peace and hope that God wants us to have, because He is so willing to pardon us of all sins which we repent of. When we are convicted of doing wrong, that is God's way of prodding us to quickly get back on the right path with Him. When we feel condemned, it is the devil's way of trying to keep us in bondage. We fight the devil most effectively when we pray according to God's word and refuse to doubt His word and His love for you. Therefore, as a child of the most high God, He gives us His authority to declare, "There is no condemnation for those who are in Christ Jesus" (Rom. 8:1). We end up being in bondage when we believe other than the truth of what God says in His word. When we believe we have not forgiven ourselves after we have repented, we doubt and deny God's ability and His pardoning grace for us; when we should know the extent of what Jesus went through that we should be pardoned. This is why we need to know His word and declare the promises of His word for us that He is faithful and just to forgive us of all sins and cleanse us from all unrighteousness (1 John 1:9). We need to have the heart and eyes of faith by believing His word rather than being led by our fickle emotions and our own understanding which is often contrary to God's word. The devil often attacks the minds of people the most, because our ungodly actions starts with wrong thinking. When we listen to his lies long enough, it feeds on our emotions, and then we forget the truth of what God actually says. Then we believe the lies of the deceiver himself. This is the old adage of his tricks, when he deceived Adam and Eve in the Garden of Eden right from the beginning. When Eve listened to his lies long enough, she forgot the simple command that God had given her when He told her what would happen if she should eat from the tree of the Knowledge of Good and Evil, which God was distinctly clear about. Because Eve listened to the lies of the enemy long enough, she was convinced to believe a lie rather than guarding her mind to keep it steadfast to what God had instructed her not to do.

God wants to prosper us in all areas of our lives because that's what He indicated when you read the epistle of 3 John 2. All too often, I hear many Christians say that they do not like or believe the prosperity gospel. Well, if that's the case, they must not like the gospel in the Bible. Prosperity is mentioned ninety-one times in the New International Version (NIV) of the Bible. This is another area where the devil robs many people because God is quite clear about delighting to prosper His children. The reason why so many people miss out on much of what God wants to do on their behalf is because they listen to the counsel of man rather than taking the time to see what God has to say about it. They fail to test the spirit to see if they line up with what God says. If people become offended about this, or disagrees to what the word says, this is where people have to examine their heart. We must remember that we need to conform and allow God to transform us to what the Bible says, not for the Bible to be molded to our liking. The Bible needs to change us, not us to change the Bible. We miss out on so much when we don't accept the divine teachings of Gods word. Another reason why many people may not want to believe in the prosperity gospel, is that they would have a guilty conscious about believing they would become greedy and developing a love of money. Just because one person is rich in finances does not mean he/she is automatically in love with money. Look at both Solomon and Abraham, whom God has richly blessed. A person with a hundred dollars in the bank may love money more than a millionaire. If we are concerned about this, we need to ask God to change our wrong motive and wrong thinking about finances because just having money is not the purpose of living the prosperous life. When God talks about being prosperous, He talks about not only money, but also being prosperous by having a healthy marriage, maintaining healthy relationships with God and with one another, living in divine health, along with being rich in wisdom, knowledge and understanding that He offers as one of the gifts of the Spirit (read 1 Cor 12:4-11). If we only consider being prosperous in relation to money, we only end up having a small piece of the whole pie. I don't know about you, but I have been passionate about helping so many hurting people, especially in Africa. I would far rather have a lot of money in order to financially help them to dig wells so more people can enjoy fresh drinking water. I would rather be able to financially support families in need of the basic necessities, help send children to school and buy them nice clothes to wear. This is the reason why we should want to prosper, is because we should want and desire to be a blessing to others which will ultimately give God the glory. It gives me greater joy when I live the prosperous life in order to be able to see others blessed from it. When I went to Zambia in 2006, I have been able to purchase many articles of clothing, blankets, mosquito nets, shoes and food. It was wonderful to see the look on peoples faces when they were overjoyed to receive these items that they so desperately needed. That is why I delight to prosper as God does, so that we are able to bless others. No wonder God says in Acts 20:35 that "It is more blessed to give than it is to receive." He encourages us to pray and ask Him to bless us indeed, for His name's sake and to be a blessing unto others. When we do, we fulfill His will and His plan. We cannot give what we don't have, and we cannot bless others if we have not been first blessed. I believe God included the prayer of Jabez in His word because He wanted us to see it for ourselves, apply it to our lives today, and He didn't want it to be just another story in the Bible. Therefore, we can declare the same prayer that Jabez prayed, "Oh, that you would bless me indeed and enlarge my territory! Let Your hand be with me, and keep me from harm so that I will not cause Thee pain," and God granted him his request (1 Chron. 4:10). It is vitally important that we see His word as His love letter to us and realize that it is His wise and loving instructions for us to live by and apply to our lives today rather than just treating the Bible as some form of a history lesson. People who treat the Bible only as a history lesson think and say that events which took place back then was only for Biblical times rather than applying His principles for us today. God reminds us that He is the same yesterday, today and forever (Heb. 13:8). I encourage you not to let the devil rob and deceive you any longer by misinterpreting the word, having pre-conceived ideas or because of what someone else says. If Jesus is our Lord, we need to let His word be our final authority despite what anyone else has to say about any issue. Let God help you put that desire in your heart, to be prosperous in all areas of your life in order to be generous to others. This is what it really means to live the prosperous life which God clearly indicates in His written word which is His perfect will!!

Chapter 12

Bondage of Traditions

When we look in the mirror in the light of His word, how do we see ourselves through God's perspective? How do we look to the outside world? It's very unfortunate that a lot of people I see walking into a worship service walk and parade themselves with a staunch look and a radiance about them that looks as though they were attending a funeral rather than a joyous worship service which we should feel privileged to gather together for. David says, "I was glad when they said unto me, let us go into the House of the Lord" (Psalm 122:1). His delight was to gather together to worship our King, Jesus. I wonder many times if people have not dealt with any hidden sin, or felt as though they have not forgiven themselves even after repenting? I believe even more so, that many "so-called Christians" do not portray the radiance of Christ because they are in bondage to following the traditions of their ancestors while forsaking God's instructions (read Mark 7:8) and also allowing pride to fill their heart because they look down on others by exalting themselves. God was pleased to justify the sinner beating his breast and crying out to God "Forgive me a sinner." At the same time, the prideful Pharisee who exalted himself, God did not justify. This is that same extreme deadly spirit of pride that caused Lucifer, whom at the beginning was considered one of God's highest angels. But because he was lifted up with pride, he became satan (prince of darkness) which God has hurled him out of heaven and will ultimately destroy him and his following angels forever (Isaiah 14:11-17).

When we delight to do God's will and delight to live for God, He doesn't impose the regulations on us of the Do's and Don'ts. God puts His laws in our hearts, so we will do what is right because we want to, not because other people say we have to do it or cannot do it. It's for God's Holy Spirit to do that and to work in the hearts of men. People judge others because of what they wear, but fail to see the heart. Whereas, our God judges the hearts of men. We need to be careful not to judge others by what we see, but we must see each other in the light of Christ, and love them as Jesus would do. We are called to be imitators of Jesus (Eph. 5:1). If we simply follow the "rules and regulations" of a specific denomination, I challenge you to ask God to compare it in the light of His word and see what He says. After all, Christ (the Word) is to be the Head of the Church, and not the spiritual hierarchy in which the leaders of the Church must be under submission to. When we delight ourselves in the Lord, He will always give us the desires of our heart, and we will continue to do what is right in His sight (Psalm 37:4). When we do the things laid out in the light of "rules and regulations," it becomes legalism, and that is not what God ever intended. If we could ever be justified by keeping a bunch of rules and regulations, we would actually be telling God that we have no need of His grace and mercy which we so desperately need.

When we carry around a staunch look or a face that shows no peace or joy, do you think for one second we will attract others to Christ? When we develop a deep love and reverence for the Lord, we will have the fear and reverence for Him as it is fitting to do so, because of who He truly is. Wisdom brightens a person's countenance (Eccl. 8:1; Ezek. 28:7). If we go around with anything but a radiant countenance of God's love on our face, we must ask God to help deal with whatever we are going through. His Holy Spirit is always there to help us and to teach us about the knowledge of having the reverent fear of the Lord in our heart. We need to truly be honest with God and confess our lack of reverential fear of Him and Godly love for one another, if this is true about us. After all, His word does explicitly say that the whole duty of man is to fear God and obey His commands (Eccl. 12:13). Be encouraged to follow God's word with the loving guidance of His Holy Spirit and you will be able to be free from the bondages of "regulations" which often are contrary to His word. We will have the peace and joy of the radiance of Christ within us because we follow Jesus, regardless of what other institutions may say or do. If we decide not to ask Him and believe that we have the answers for our circumstances, then how can we call Him Lord if we don't ever acknowledge Him to give us the right answers and lead us on the right path? Jesus asks, "How can you call Me Lord when you do not do the things I command you to do?" (Luke 6:46).

I encourage you to ask God to see if there are any wrong paths you may be following, and invite Him to reveal the truth which will set you free (John 8:32). Another one of the many promises of God is to acknowledge Him in all your ways, and He will direct your paths (Proverbs 3:6). As this scripture indicates, although He promises to direct our path, our responsibility lies in the fact that we need to acknowledge our need of His help first and foremost. He wants to teach us to open our hearts and our arms to Him because He works most effectively when we humble ourselves by inviting Him in to work on our behalf.

Chapter 13

DO WE BELIEVE IN MAN OR GOD?

Do we take heed over what man says we are, or do we see who we are in the light of God's word? Many times in my past, a person would mention something negative about me or about my limited abilities and/or inability(ies). I had to work for someone who was comparable to a dictator, and of course, there weren't many words of encouragement for myself, no matter what. I could have believed his lies and felt sorry for myself, which would be followed by developing bitterness, envy, and perhaps hatred to brew within me from his accusations. When I think of someone who accuses someone else, I think that they are closely related to the devil himself, because he is depicted as the accuser of the brethren. When the devil accuses, he cannot face the truth because he is a liar, and no truth is found in him. When people start accusing, they are being molded in believing a lie by being led by the one whom they are following as their bad example. They can never face up to the truth of taking responsibility and speaking responsibly. The only time I've heard of an accusation it was indicated as a "false accusation." I have never heard of any accusation as being a "true accusation." It's one thing to accuse, but entirely another thing to correct or admonish. When a person accuses, they do not do it with the hope of benefiting others, but they revel in the outcome of destruction in order to exalt themselves, while someone who gently corrects is used of God in the hopes of benefiting the hearer.

When I read the word of God, He often says something totally different from what any of our accusers would say of us. For instance, in Phil. 4:13, He says, "I can do all things through Christ who strengthens me," as opposed to someone who might say something totally the opposite. I definitely choose to believe what the word of God says about me. Why do we often get so caught up with man's so-called influence of opinions about us?

I believe the problem is threefold. First, we attempt to be man pleasers and we want to be accepted by man's opinion instead of pleasing God. When people strive to please other people and strive to receive their acceptance through another human, they often become frustrated. Then before too long, they develop an inferiority complex because they didn't meet "their approval" or achieve their level of expectation to be accepted.

Secondly, many people accept other people's opinions over what God clearly says in His word. I had a boss say to me that I would never be able to manage a retail store. I could have been defeated by what he said, but I chose to believe God's word of encouragement instead. Needless to say, after I took over the operation of a retail outlet the following year at a military station, I was reminded that I had operated the retail outlet better than it had ever been done in the past. I don't take any credit whatsoever without first giving God the glory. The point is that we can believe a lie from human lips when they speak discouragement or false accusations. That's when we become defeated. Or else, we can go to God's word, believe what He says, and be encouraged. We then vow not to be defeated from the lies of the deceiver himself.

Thirdly, we may be in bondage of maintaining our reputation, when we should be more concerned about our character. I recently heard it stated perfectly, that our reputation is how we view ourselves according to what others say, and our character is defined by viewing ourselves by caring about what God thinks of us, despite what others may think.

We have a choice. Then why do we see ourselves as others may see us if it's negative? We need to see ourselves as God sees us. After all, He is God and He alone is the only One who knows all things. So why would we judge ourselves by what others think or say about us? The Biblical verse in 1 Cor. 2:15 is a good example of the Lord's illustration that we do not have to be subjected to any man's judgment. Does that person revere himself as God, or does he think he is all-knowing? Should we believe him? If God says, "We are more than conquerors through Christ who loves us," and someone says something else, who are you going to believe? If someone says something about you that is contrary to God's word, then they are simply being used by the devil who is nothing but a "foul-mouthed liar." We have to remember, however, that we need to be angry with sin itself, and not the sinner. After all, the sinner has been blinded by the "god of this world," whom satan is depicted as (2 Cor. 4:4). The only reason why satan is called the god of this world, is because the world has made him their god.

Everyone has some form of god they idolize or follow whether they realize it or not. If we are not following the true living God according to the Bible, then we are following another god, which may include materialism, idolizing people, money, being consumed in work/sports, or coveting anything else that would replace God, whom should be first in each person's life. That is why He alone has a right to declare that He is a jealous God (Josh. 24:9). If anyone speaks contrary to God's truth, then it must mean that they are speaking as a liar and a deceiver because they are speaking other than what is the truth, which is the only standard found in God's word. Start turning a deaf ear to the lies of human lips who try to judge you and persevere to declare the promises and the encouraging Word of what God says about you! I guarantee that you will like yourself much better when you see yourself as God sees you and says who you are in the light and truth of His word.

When we are on our guard about this issue, we will not become a victim of the enemy by harboring anger and bitterness, which, when it becomes established as a root will cause many to become defiled (Heb. 12:15) This is one of the devices satan uses to trip up many Christians. That is why I cannot emphasize the importance of knowing the enemy, and knowing how to handle the Word of God effectively to defeat our enemy every time.

Chapter 14

HATING WHAT GOD HATES

The enemy often softens various terms to make them seem more tolerable today, and they may be highly offensive towards God. Satan is deceiving society more and more by using the term "politically correct" to pull us further away from having the same mindset as God. An example is, if Jesus were "politically correct," He would never have called the Pharisees "Hypocrites" or a "Brood of Vipers." If there was anyone on earth who ever spoke the truth in love, it was Jesus. However, we must take precautions if we are to speak as Christ did, because our motive has to be girded with love, just as God himself is love.

A lot of Christians would admit that hate is a harsh word and many would say that we should never hate anything, even sin. If that were so, why does God say He hates sin? God tells us in His word we are to hate evil like He hates evil, and cling to what is good. Have you ever noticed how Jesus doesn't pat any term or powder it up to cover up any use of words? He says it like it is. For instance, when we say people are not telling the truth, Jesus says that person is lying. When moneychangers were in the house of God, Jesus didn't politely tell them they were not supposed to do that there. He overturned the tables and drove them out. At the same time, Jesus never allowed anger to control Him in any circumstances.

When He says hate, He means hate and not "dislike," "tolerate," etc. In other words, we are to hate sin and not just "dislike" it. Jesus may have often seemed harsh, but He always was motivated by love. Therefore, whatever we do in the name of Christ, we need to be certain we are always motivated by His love and allow His love to work within us. The enemy has allowed us to become compromisers of God's word, and instead of us hating evil what God calls evil, we begin to "dislike" evil. Little by little, when people have become lax about hating what God hates and have become "dislikers," what we once disliked about any certain agenda, we eventually became "tolerant." When people who have become tolerant do not share the same thoughts as God does, it will eventually become "acceptance," whereby many things that God explicitly states that He hates and is an abomination towards Him, has now become the acceptable practice in today's society. People didn't one day adamantly follow God and have the same mindset and just decide to go the complete opposite way by "accepting" a wrongful act the following day. It started with allowing the enemy coming in a subtle manner and working little by little, so that what is now "acceptable" was previously "tolerable" and what was tolerable, once was "dislike." When we hate what God hates, such as homosexuality, a lying tongue, a proud look, adultery, witchcraft, idolatry, etc., we will be certain to stand more firm in doing what is right and believing what is right because we share the same mindset as God does. What God says and does is right! This is what holiness is about—when we love what God loves and hate what God hates. Without holiness, we are told we will never see God (Hebrews 12:14b). Unfortunately, many Christians have allowed themselves to be an advocate of human rights and accept agendas such as homosexuality and same sex marriage. They first of all have allowed themselves to tolerate an agenda, even though it contradicts God's word. They failed to value the high standard God intends for us to keep. So if God says that witchcraft is an abomination to Him, it should equally be an abomination for us. Like I mentioned earlier, society turns away from God slowly, little by little, rather than doing a complete turnaround. That is why satan is called the "angel of light" because he masquerades like one, deceiving those who are unaware of his schemes. This is another huge area that people mention that we need to change with the times. God warns His people in 2 Tim. 4:4 "they will turn their ears away from the truth and turn aside to myths." God will never change His mind because His counsel is perfect. If God ever changes His mind about any issue, He would not remain perfect, and His word, whom Christ is identified as (read John1:1,14) would no longer be our authority. That is why man is so unstable and God's word will always remain stable. That is why there is a constant danger of following and believing the vain philosophies of man, especially when it contradicts what God says in His word.

When the devil has finally taken a mile in your life, it was all started by you giving him an inch. We are told not to even give him a foothold or to open a door to him. I have been blessed to say the prayer, where I frequently ask God to help me love the things He loves and hate the things He Himself hates. If you love justice like God does, you will equally hate injustice as God does. If you love holiness like God does, you will hate sin as God does and not ever come to just disliking sin. If you love others like God tells us to love, you will hate "indifference." If you love His word, you will hate all false pretenses that oppose His word. I like what David says in Psalm 119: "Because I love Your commands more than gold, more than pure gold and because I consider your precepts right, I hate every wrong path." When we value His word as Peter said to Jesus about His word being the only way to eternal life, we also end up hating the ways of what will otherwise lead us to destruction.

When Jesus was talking about God and money, He said, "You will love one and hate the other." When He says you will love one and hate the other, that is exactly what He means. You will notice that He uses the measure of extreme here and does not identify it in softer terms. He means what He says and nothing less!

Not only unbelievers, but even many Christians have indicated to me that much of the events that happened in the Bible was for the past and it's not pertinent for the present. Believing otherwise is listening to the lies of the devil, who is considered a deceiver who leads the whole world astray (read Rev. 12:9). Let us not be deceived by the subtle ways of the enemy. Ask God to help us love what He loves and hate what He hates. When we do that to the degree that He does, we do what is right and just because God and the instruction of His word is perfect. To benefit in our love for God, we should hate any false and compromising ways to what God says in

His word. If we truly love Him, by loving His word, the enemy will find it harder to deceive us and we will be less likely to compromise His loving word. We will be able to keep our feet planted to stay and be able to stand firm having our "houses"(lives) built upon the "Rock" which is Christ Jesus Himself (Deut. 32:4,15; 1 Cor. 10:4).

Chapter 15

BEING STUBBORN FOR JESUS

I have often wondered why people in general are stubborn and don't take a stand about the things of this world. Christians are not stubborn when taking a stand for the truth about God's word. I use myself as an example of this from the past. When I reflect on my past and what I have learned, I believe I have grown stronger in the Lord because of adverse conditions. We can only know how strong we are in the Lord when we are faced with trials which would tempt us to doubt God's word for us, doubt His love for us, and doubt ourselves of who God says we are and says about Himself. When we do not exercise our faith and remain strong in the Lord, we become weaker and more vulnerable. God brought a thought to my mind as I was mentioning this. This past week, my rear wiper on my vehicle's window ceased working. It happened to be a very minor job. However, the mechanic said that I should operate it at least once a day (sunshine or rain) to keep it in good working condition. What had happened was that the wiper was hardly being used and when I needed to use the wiper, it was hardly operating at all. It wasn't able to do its job as it should have. The reason was a lack of "exercise" and that's why it eventually ceased. Some of the physically strongest elderly people living are the ones who exercise frequently. It reminded me of when we don't frequently exercise our spirit, operate our faith, and trust in Him when we are tried, we become weaker and cease to be as effective. When we are faced with opposition (spiritual, physical or mental), God has helped me to be stubborn to refuse to doubt Him, refuse to believe the lies and deception of the devil, refuse to compromise God's word, or refuse to give up believing God or doing His will. When the world would seem stubborn to stand against the will of God, we need to be equally stubborn to stand against the enemy and refuse to be deceived by his lies and be stubborn to believe in God's pure and Holy Word. By accepting His grace after having gone through trials, God has truly helped me to become a stronger Christian. When I have been faced with temptations to doubt God's promises, which satan himself continually attacks our minds, I have to be more determined than ever, to refuse to doubt God, His word, His love, or believing He has not answered my prayers by the present circumstances. I have learned to believe Him no matter what it takes. Determine in your heart and audibly say, "If God said it, I believe it, and that settles it." That is the childlike faith that God is most pleased with.

Believing and refusing to doubt areas in our prayer life, such as praying for the salvation of unsaved family members, refusing to doubt the promises of God when I do according to His will, and knowing that He answers prayer when we believe and pray according to His will (1 John 5:14-15). When the devil throws his darts at you, you need to rise up and take the shield of faith to knock down his darts of false accusations by speaking what God says in His word in Isaiah 54:17. The spoken Word is what is compared to a sword that is the offensive weapon to attack the enemy when we are informed to wear our full spiritual armor (Eph. 6:10-16). The devil doesn't just throw darts at you, he is subtle in his ways. That's why he is compared to a snake. He is that wolf in sheep's clothing that the Bible indicates that he masquerades as an angel of light (2 Cor. 11:14). For we know that there is absolutely no light in him. Therefore, he is a counterfeit. He will often try to get you to question God, just like he did right from the beginning with Eve. We have to tell the devil, "The Lord rebuke you" (Jude 9), "For it is written." Speak the written Word and say nothing more than that. May God help you to use this opportunity to become stronger for the Lord and refuse to give up, because the enemy is already defeated and we need to remind our enemy of that and let him know that we know he is a defeated enemy. Christ Himself said, "We have victory through Christ Jesus" (1 Cor. 15:57), whereby He didn't say we will have, but we already have victory!

Also, we are more than conquerors through Christ who loves us (Rom. 8:37)! He speaks in the present tense, and not in the future tense. When satan would have us believe because we see the evidence, we need to take a stand against the enemy and say to him as Christ did, "For it is written," because the devil hates the the truth of God's word, the blood of Jesus, the name of Jesus and our unshakable faith in Him because he knows he is defeated. Christ used the word, which defeated the enemy every time. The devil is nothing but a counterfeit and a liar because there is no truth in him (John 8:44). Paul didn't become a strong apostle just by chance. He was strong because of the adversity he endured by trusting in God. He refused to give up his hope which was in Christ Jesus. He exercised his mind and heart to believe what God says, to know the love of God for him, and to use his authority he knew God gives to each of His children. It's the same way in the physical realm. If we are expected to be physically strong, we must exercise our physical strength to be able to handle certain types of work. Therefore, if we expect to be spiritually strong, we must exercise spiritually by being in the Word, declaring His promises and love for us, being alone with God, praying and meditating His word, which brings eternal life.

Paul endured many hardships, but it cannot be compared to the glory he now continues to experience having been faithful to the One who is loving and faithful towards us (Rom. 8:18). When opposition seems to overwhelm us, remember it only took 300 of Gideon's mighty army to defeat thousands of the enemy forces—the Midianites (Judges 7). We need to be still and audibly declare the hand of God to be against our spiritual enemy, and let God fight our battles (2 Chron. 20:15). The battles we win are the ones we let God fight as we humble ourselves before Him, pray, and praise Him for the victory. The works that we do that Jesus tells us are that we must believe unto the One whom God has sent (John 6:29).

Therefore, we need to be stubborn against the lies of the devil and refuse to give up in what God has promised us according to His word. If God said it, refuse to doubt it! That's the childlike faith God says He is really pleased with. "And above all, take up the shield of faith with which you can extinguish all the flaming arrows of the evil one" (Eph. 6:16).

Chapter 16

Declaring War on the Real Enemy

One of the devastating tools our enemy (the devil) continues to use effectively today is for us to doubt who we really are in Christ Jesus. My heart breaks when I see so many Christians continually confessing that they are being defeated and tormented by the devil and his forces because many have been believing a lie and doubting who God says we are when we first received Christ into our lives as our Lord and personal savior. God tells us that if we are His children, then we are joint heirs with Jesus (Rom. 8:17). We have been bought at the greatest expense of God Himself by giving His very life for us and shedding His blood for us.

In our time of prayer, each of us needs to go back to what God says and declare for ourselves, "If my people who are called by my name, will humble themselves, turn from their wicked ways, pray and seek His face, then will God hear from heaven, forgive all our sins and heal our lands (2 Chron. 7:14). It makes me realize that the tormentor himself should be the "tormented one" when we realize who we are in Christ and the authority that God has given to us. We have the privilege of being called the sons of God and declaring the promises of His word for us. Several things that the devil hates is the blood, the word of God and our unshakable faith in Christ. When Christ was tempted, He declared the word of God and the devil could not tempt Him again with the same temptation. He has given us all the power of using the weapons of warfare to live in victory. The minute Jesus said on the cross of Calvary, "It is finished," the devil knew he was defeated at that time. One of the things that the devil uses when we doubt who we are in Christ, is when we sin, we allow the devil to torment us by reminding us of the sins we have committed. We need to stand and declare His word, which is His promise for us that we are able to be free from carrying the burdens of our past and know with the assurance that God has forgiven us our sins in the "sea of forgetfulness." We often see ourselves failing because we see ourselves less than perfect. God Himself knows we will not ever be perfect, until what is perfect has arrived to receive us unto Himself (1 Cor. 13:10).

Another area where we need to start declaring war is to stand united one with another. We have to declare war on the issues that the devil uses to come against us like division, strife, criticism, apathy, lukewarmness and being compromisers of God's word and His will. When we turn from His will and do our own will, we suffer the consequences of not living the victorious and best possible Christian life God has called for us. Whenever saints of God are in division with doctrine, they need to cease striving and encourage each other with gentleness to get on our knees to seek God's direction. After all, it is His Spirit that guides us into all truth (John 16:13), not our argumentative ways. God has richly helped me when I seek Him, and have asked Him to reveal His truth to me. I am told to receive it with joy in my heart and rebuke, reject, and hate anything that would compromise receiving the fullness of the absolute, and uncompromising truth of His word. We can be compared to King David, a man after God's own heart as declared in Psalm 119:127, 128 "Because I love your commands more than gold, more than pure gold, and because I consider all your precepts right, I hate every wrong path." You will notice that it doesn't simply say "dislike," but hates! We are right to hate anything that God (who is pure and holy) also hates and doesn't approve of. God has also inspired me with this to come together in unity, because there is power in unity. He also states that no kingdom can stand when it is divided against itself.

When you read Acts chapters 1, 2 and 3, you will notice when God's people came together in one place, having one accord (being in agreement) to lift up the name of Jesus, He was able to perform wonders and demonstrate His power through the people. I believe God is all powerful simply because the trinity of the Godhead is in perfect unity. If we would come together in unity, fight the enemy, and use the weapons of warfare, hating evil, loving others, hating what God hates, loving what God loves, keeping our focus on His love for us and what He has done for us, the power of God would move through His people like never before. The devil will also try to trip us up when we question God, and ask why does this evil happen? We need to keep focused on how much He truly loves us by His willingness to go to the cross for us and die the shameful death on the cross and shed His blood and take the punishment we deserved upon Himself. We need to earnestly pray that each of us with God's help, can break down the walls of division, denominationalism, becoming islands among ourselves and join forces as one in the kingdom of God seeking to do His good and perfect will. You will notice that one of the ways when we are prone to defeat is when we become like islands among ourselves. The result of this is that sooner or later, when various groups become separated, there is a very distinct possibility that there will be individuals feeling left outside, and all alone. That is when wolves make their attack on the sheep; when they can try to separate a lonely sheep away from the pack. This is comparable to the Christian who will be much more prone to the devil's attack, when they feel isolated, because He mentions that we benefit when we are down and have someone to help us up, but woe to the one who has no one else to help him (Eccl. 4:10). Real power is present when unity of a body is present. This is why I believe the Godhead is perfect in power, because God the father, Jesus the son, and the Holy Spirit are always in perfect unity.

Jesus mentions to His disciples that a kingdom will never be able to stand when it is divided against one another. That is why God desires so much that we become and remain united one with another. It's like trying to sever the natural body. That is why we need to do all we can to keep the unity with one another in order to be most effective when dealing with the weapons of our warfare. After all, Jesus mentions that, "Whatsoever you do unto the least of my children, you do unto me" (Matt. 25:31-45). Depending how we get along with one another will determine our relationship with Jesus. To know how good you get along with people you normally do not fellowship with, or people you would rather not associate with, is the amount you love Jesus. No one can ever say with outstretched arms that they love Jesus that much, if they are not willing to say the very same about others. The best chapters that talk about our loving relationship with Jesus depending on our love for one another is found throughout the three epistles of John. I would highly encourage you now to slowly read through these three epistles of John and let the Word feed and bless your spirit. Remember to give additional thought to what you read in order to benefit the most from God's word.

Therefore, when God gives us His word and we covet His word and instructions for us, this is the very key to reaping the greatest rewards for all eternity. When we ask in prayer to covet His word for us, we will also hate compromising His word, because that is another vice that satan uses against the saints. When we compromise the value of His word in our lives, we lose the fullness of His power in our lives because it's His word alone. When we live by and speak His word, we become empowered by His Spirit in His divine presence.

We fight most effectively against the principalities and powers that are at work against us, by confessing our dependence on God and remain humble before Him. Jesus tells us that we are to, "Act justly, love mercy, and walk humbly before God (Micah 6:8). When God gives us His instructions, it is not because it is a "good thing to do," but it is acknowledging the truth about requiring our dependency upon Him. We simply deceive ourselves from knowing the truth when we do not accept the fullness of His word for us. That is why Jesus always spoke with power, because He Himself didn't speak idly for argument's sake, but because He always spoke the truth. By knowing the truth and accepting the very truth of His word, we are set free from any form of deception and having any false hope the devil might use by causing us to doubt and compromise any of His word. The greatest sin of all is the sin of unbelief. You will notice that there are seven things that are an abomination to Him. Notice that unbelief is near the top of this particular agenda (Rev. 21:7-8). When people do not believe, that's when God is unable to do anything. Just like Jesus was not able to do any miracles in His hometown because of unbelief (Matt. 13:58).

We need to have a deep knowing and understanding that we will receive the goodness of His grace towards us when we truly humble ourselves, seek His guidance, seek His face and know with assurance that He truly loves us in a deeper way than anyone can understand. Who can truly understand the love of God? I compare myself to Jonah, when he hoped that God would condemn Ninevah because of their wickedness. However, God refrains from destroying them, and has mercy on this nation, unlike the lack of mercy Jonah had towards this city. There is no one on earth who can't thank God for being merciful towards us when we so very often deserve otherwise.

Lack of being merciful is one of the many strategies of the devil. He knows how powerless the church is when division is present, and lack of sincere prayers are lifted up when we do not keep one another in prayer. When Jesus tells us to be angry and sin not, the things we need to be angry about include areas such as strife, division, criticism, judgmental spirit, indifference and any actions that do not bear the fruit of righteousness. Therefore, we need to be angry against ungodliness, not people. The devil would not like it more than for people to come against other people when the devil himself and his fallen angels are the ones influencing others to do their dirty work. He gets the minds of the people to come against each other rather than to come against the kingdom of darkness.

Be encouraged to know that God's Spirit is always there to divinely help when we pray, and do according to His will. When we do, we win the war against our enemy because when we use His word, it's the only way that defeats satan. Of all the armor God talks about in Ephesians 6:10-16, the Sword (His word) is the only offensive armor that attacks our enemy; the other pieces of armor help protect or defend us. With our prayers and love for His word and genuine love for one another, we are able to defeat the enemy in the mighty precious name of Jesus. The promise of His word declares for us that, "We are more than conquerors through Christ who loves us" (Rom. 8:37).

SECTION III

Nourishment For Your Soul

Chapter 17

HEART OF THE MATTER

Have you ever wondered why something didn't go right and negative circumstances resulted? It's not so much that I have been on the receiving end, because I have no control over the actions of people. I do, however, have to control how I'm going to react. God expects us to have self-control, because that is one of the fruits of the Spirit we are commanded to bear. Proverbs 25:28 states that, "A person who lacks self-control is like a city with broken down walls." When the world would believe that strength comes from physical power, God tells us that a person who can control his own spirit is better than the one who is able to overthrow a city (Proverbs 16:32).

Most of the problems I have had to deal with in the past were the fault of the wrong condition of my heart. It was what you call the "heart of the matter." I have meditated on the verse in Psalm 51:10, "Create in me a clean heart, O Lord, and renew a right and steadfast spirit within me." When I ask God and ponder why and how come, I receive positive results when I trust in the Lord for His answers. However, I remain negative and bitter when I continue to ask God the question, "Why" or "How come, God?" while I don't trust Him with any situation. Then my question to Him remains and I begin to doubt and fret.

I have experienced that dark deeds are continued throughout the world, mainly because of the corrupted conditions of the heart of every individual, which I was no exception. When I see that most of my past problems were due to the condition of my heart, I have prayed the prayer of the Psalmist in Psalm 51:10-13 and asked the dear Lord to cleanse me thoroughly and purge me from deep within, that I would radiate His likeness and be His light.

We often may not be able to let His light shine through us because we have dimmed His light from un-repented sins. We may not have asked God to cleanse us from deep within, or asked God to create in us a clean heart and have a right and willing spirit within us. When we realize that His word brings forth life and that He delights to give us life in abundance, we will benefit most by wanting to be submissive to His loving word which is the only way to everlasting life. I know God has honored my prayers when I've asked Him to delight my ways by conforming to His ways and help me develop a Godly character more and more each day. Jesus is considered to be the Great Physician, who is able to do a work in our heart if we will ask Him and invite Him to do so. I hope you will be blessed knowing the freedom of walking in the light of His word and encouraging yourself and others in the Lord.

Chapter 18

WATCHING WHAT WE SAY

When I take the time to learn more from scripture, I realize the power of spoken words. When we speak words one to another, or about one another, it has the power to build and edify or to tear down and destroy. That is why Jesus says to let our words be few (Matt. 12:35-37). With every idle word we speak, we are going to give an account because of the power and effects of it. When you read James 3:6, it indicates that the flames of hell are enlarged when people speak blasphemy and words that do not edify. Also, we often become loose with our words and don't realize the significance of their meaning. As an example, I occasionally meet Christians who use the term "luck" or "wish." I would ask and discourage you from using those words loosely because those words are a source that portrays a situation that would occur in your favor by chance or coincidence. The God we serve is a sovereign God who is in complete control. Remember that your heavenly Father knows each sparrow that falls to the ground, so nothing, even minor is out of His control. He also knows the number of hairs on your head! If we truly believe God to be in perfect control and that He is able to perform as He says He can, we would never consider the fact that we need to make a wish or consider ourselves "lucky" when we, who are God-fearing people understand that the whole world is in His hands. When you say "luck" or "wish" to someone, it is like you are relying on a source or power of chance to help you rather than relying on the One whom we ought to rely on and lean on. Nowhere does God admonish us to make a wish or consider anyone to be lucky. However, He blesses them, knowing that the hand of God, His Father is upon them to indeed bless them. In the word, Christ never made a wish, but mentions the fact that He prayed often.

When we believe that something happens by "chance" or "coincidence," we deny the sovereign power, and the omniscient and omnipotent attributes of the awesome creator we are to worship. I like to consider the word "lucky." Notice that if you delete the "K" and change the "y" to an "i," it spells the first four letters of lucifer! In comparison, it's like changing the letters of santa and moving the letter "n" to the end of the word to spell satan. I don't think there is anything wrong with acknowledging innocent "jolly old Saint Nick," but when santa becomes an idol and takes us away from focusing our hearts to honor Jesus instead, it truly grieves God, because our God has every right to be called a jealous God. It's only the trinity of God who is worthy to be worshipped. He is the only One who was that perfect sacrifice who made it possible for us to have eternal life. Then again, is this not the main strategy of satan to turn your focus from Jesus towards other "idols?" People who idolize something or someone else other than God Himself have initially put their primary focus on things, which, later on, become their "god" that satisfies their wants and needs. When you read Exodus 20:1-6, you will notice that two of the first three commandments of God had been violated when we have other gods we cherish more than the One and only true living God. There is absolutely no other way that we may be saved, except through Christ Jesus. It's just another reminder of the subtle ways of how our enemy works. What may seem harmless to man is what the devil often uses. In Proverbs 14:12 God tells us that "There is a way that seems right to a man, but in the end it leads to death." So what seems harmless to man, satan is often effective because he is a master deceiver.

Secondly, when we speak to admonish, exhort, or to correct someone, we need to be sensitive to the Holy Spirit's leading. If we allow our tongues to be too loose, our words can have a detrimental affect on each other. If we are not careful and sensitive also to the needs of others, the very words we speak can bring discouragement to the hearer. Negative words spoken to others can fester within them, and the results can be disastrous. This allows the enemy to rob, kill and eventually destroy their very lives. Several years ago someone mentioned to me that words were spoken to a person that indicated she was too fat. She took it to heart and that person became so self-conscious about herself that she became anorexic which ended up taking her very life. This would not have had its detrimental effect had someone not spoken those hurtful words which ultimately destroyed her life.

Paul tells us that we need to exhort one another and to correct a fellow Christian who is living in sin. But when we do, we need to have the gentle spirit of God by having the compassion of correcting them in the love of God and continually to be mindful of God's love for them. When we don't, we become critical because they don't meet up with our expectations of whom they should be. God reminds those who think that way and questions them about how many times they didn't meet up with God's expectations? Many more times, I, myself, can say that I didn't measure up to God's expectations, and yet, He lovingly encourages me. When I remember how merciful He continues to be towards me, I'm reminded to do the same by being merciful to others. After all, it should be our goal and desire to bring out the best in others. We rarely do that by being critical and having a judgmental spirit. There are times we need to be constructive in our criticism in order to correct someone, but it should soon be followed by a word of encouragement. When we encourage one another in the Lord, we are not simply saying a lot of words just to be nice, but when our words of encouragement line up with God's word, there is great power. His word is the absolute truth that gives us victory over any matter or concerns we may have. When we grew up as little children, we would say in ignorance that, "Sticks and stones may break our bones, but names can never hurt us." I would dare say that many times, healing from a physical wound such as being hit by sticks and stones takes place much faster than any hurtful words can. Sometimes, people have suffered through the remaining years of their lives because of the destructive impact those words had on them. The tongue is an unruly vessel, yet it is compared to a small rudder that steers the huge ship, and so it is with our tongues. Though it is small, it directs our course in life and the untamed tongue causes the fires of hell to enlarge itself (James 3:4–9). It's a serious matter that should be considered when sadly, most Christians do not take it seriously regarding the destructive effects of what our words can bring to others.

God admonishes the truth in His word about when words are many, sin is present (Eccl. 5:3). That doesn't mean that we can't talk very much, but the fact that gossip and slander will be more prevalent, and more words will come out of our mouths that are not edifying or encouraging to the hearers if we do not give thought about what we speak. God lovingly warns us that we will give an account for every idle word that proceeds out of the mouth. When we are determined to keep our mind on the things of what God wants us to think about, we will be able to guard our hearts. Luke 6:45 tells us that "Out of the overflow of his heart, the mouth speaks. Therefore, it starts in the mindset of believers, and we need to acknowledge God to help us maintain our correct thinking. Remember, God wants us to include Him and acknowledge Him in all things, because He knows He is the only One who can truly help us. However, we need to ask and acknowledge our dependency upon His help. Whenever we acknowledge Him in all our ways, His promise to us is that He will direct our paths (Proverbs 3:6).

Jesus answered the Pharisees and Sadducees after they questioned Him about not washing His hands before eating. Jesus replied and said that this is not what defiles a man, but it is the unclean words that come out of the heart that defiles a man. It's a real trick of the enemy how often he used the Pharisees, Sadducees and the teachers of the law to ensnare them with many idle words the devil would have them use, in which they are presently giving an account for (Matt. 12:36). Jesus teaches us in Mark 11:23 that what we believe and confess, will come to pass. Death and life are in the power of the tongue (Proverbs 18:21). Therefore, it is imperative that we cultivate our thinking and speaking with the life giving blessings of God's word. When people believe and speak negatively, they are being contrary to God's word. They are being deceived and being robbed by the devil because they fail to believe and speak the encouraging truth of God's word into their own lives and the lives of other souls. We often are our own worst enemy when we speak negatively towards ourselves. When we do, we become ensnared by our words. In Proverbs 18:20:21, God tells us that "from the fruit of his mouth, a man's stomach is filled; with the harvest from his lips, he is satisfied. The tongue has the power of life and death, and those who love it will eat its fruit." Is it any wonder that people who consistently speak negatively live exactly the way they speak? If this is so, then why don't people start to speak the encouraging promises of God's word for themselves instead?

With God's help, we can speak words of life, edification and encouragement to ourselves and one to another, when we line up with what God says in His word. Unfortunately, this is contrary to what the world does. This is what makes us different from the world. Although we live in the world, we do not have to be part of the world system. Be encouraged to live in the higher standard that God has called us to live. He is always willing and able with His outstretched arms, reaching down from heaven, and He will lift us up when we humble ourselves before Him.

Chapter 19

GODLY SORROW VS. WORLDLY SORROW

This is a topic that you should consider seriously. Between the two, the results bring forth either life or death. Since it is such a magnificent difference in the eternal consequences, it is therefore important to know what is meant by this. When you read 2 Cor. 7:10, the word indicates that having Godly sorrow brings forth life and having worldly sorrow brings forth death. The Lord has shown me two examples of the causes of worldly sorrow versus godly sorrow, and the negative effects of having worldly sorrow as opposed to having Godly sorrow. In one aspect, I believe a result of having worldly sorrow stems from putting your hopes and trust in worldly affairs such as your job, the economy, the government, the stock market, your portfolio (money), trusting in other people to be there for you all the time, or other earthly comparisons. When we put our trust and hopes in worldly matters, sooner or later, it/they will fail you, regardless. Not if, but when it/they do fail you, you become bitter, frustrated, and angry. Tension rises and that results in un-forgiveness. This leads to worldly sorrow because you put your hope and trust into something that sooner or later will fail instead of putting your hope and trust into someone whom will never fail you which is Christ Jesus.

Sometimes people may think God has failed them, but when I look back, God knew exactly what He was doing in my life. He knew exactly how I needed to be liberated from earthly bondages by going through some rough valleys. Even though I went through rough times, I can truly say He never has failed me yet and He never will! In addition, when we have worldly sorrow, it is also a result of being self-conscious. In other words, if someone has offended you, a person who has worldly sorrow will look at themselves and want to get even. Therefore, envy, bitterness, and jealousy rages within them and they alone suffer because of it. They will say, "Look what has happened to me"! This is also the result from having pride and worrying about "self" image. However, a person who has been chastised or scorned, but is a godly person who has developed godly sorrow, will understand the big picture. They will see the tormentor being a pitiful victim of the real enemy (the devil). They will not be consumed with self, but will demonstrate what Jesus Himself said when He was being crucified and Stephen said when he was being stoned to death (Acts 7:59, 60). They both said, "Father forgive them for they know not what they do." What a difference! They didn't see themselves as a victim, but they saw the oppressors as the real victim! We need to understand, if only our oppressors knew what was really happening, they would immediately bow before God almighty and repent within seconds. But they have been blinded by the deceiver himself, because the natural man is blinded by the real warfare being fought in the spiritual realm (1 Cor. 2:14). We who are spiritually alive are able to see this. The enemies of God and His people are so blinded by their father, the devil, that they often believe they are justified by the hideous and abominable acts committed by them, not knowing they will give an account in severity far greater than the justice system this world could ever give. Therefore, both Jesus and Stephen see the devastation of the oppressors of the eternal damnation that faces them and they felt sorry for them instead of feeling sorry for themselves. This is the real difference between being like the world or being like Jesus. The difference is life or death! I think from that, it is vital to teach on this issue.

I encourage you to pray and be so full of Jesus that the enemy will never be able to deal with your "self" and he will hate to be around you. When satan sees a person being so "self-conscious," he takes advantage simply because someone who is extremely self-conscious is more concerned about their reputation than caring about what kind of representative they are to God and to others. When you love God and live according to His word, the devil sees Jesus in you, and he quickly flees. You will often notice this is why many ungodly people oppose Christians, because the devil who controls their lives cannot stand to be around those who live according to the truth about Jesus. We have become a stench to those who are perishing, but a sweet fragrance to those who are in Christ Jesus (2 Cor. 2:15). The devil hates the Truth (Jesus), because he knows he is defeated by the truth of God's Holy Word. That is why it is so important to understand, appropriate, believe and speak the truth of His word into our lives.

Chapter 20

Reaping What You Sow

When you read the principles of God's word, you will notice that Jesus mentions about reaping what you sow. It's the same principles applied to the natural realm. When a farmer wants to grow tomatoes, he will plant tomato seeds. If he wants to yield corn, then he will have to plant corn seeds. Whatever seeds he plants will determine what kind of crop he will harvest. Additionally, the quality of the crop depends on how we take care of it. If we cultivate the ground, pull out the weeds, the suckers, and water the ground, the quality of the produce will be much better than simply planting seeds and doing nothing about taking care of it during its growth. This past summer, I had a couple of trees in our backyard which the foliage on one of the trees looked rather bleak, and the apple tree barely produced any fruit. Before I decided to cut down one of the trees that had very little foliage on it, I decided to prune a lot of the dead branches off both trees. It was amazing to see the difference it made. The tree soon came into full bloom like never before and the branches on the apple tree were so full of fruit that I had never seen the branches hanging down with the weight of that much fruit. The same thing applies to our spiritual growth. If we are to benefit fully and bear much fruit as God expects of us, we first need to be attached to the vine by desiring a rich relationship with Him and our dependency on Him (John 15:4, 5). Then we must pull the spiritual weeds and suckers from our lives that saps our energy. Have you ever noticed that when we sin, we are literally drained of energy and we lack the joy and peace we could be having by keeping in right standing with God. We need to purposefully do what is contrary to what the world does, by rooting out any bitterness, jealousy, critical and judgmental attitudes and replacing them with His loving kindness, to act justly, to love mercy, and to walk humbly before God (Micah 6:8). When we pull out the weeds of sin in our lives first, we have to be certain to replace them with the purity of His word. If we only cleanse our lives and don't fill it back up with the goodness of His word, we will be worse off because what has been emptied will eventually get filled with something worse than before. Take a look at the scripture of Matt. 12:43-45, and notice how a person is worse off than before simply because they never did anything to feed their inner man with God's spirit in the first place. That means sooner or later, if we live our lives as an empty vessel, when we are not careful to fill our spirit with God's word, then it gets filled with destructive, sinful thoughts and deeds, which will cause us to be much worse off than before. Just as weeds often pop up, we need to do the same with the "spiritual weeds" in our lives by pulling them out of our lives constantly.

To gain a deeper understanding about the concept of sowing and reaping a good harvest, we need to understand that the seed is the Word of God (Matt. 13:20), and the Bible is a bag of seeds. God created man out of the dust of the earth, so we originally came from the earth. To compare this with nature, for a type of plant to grow, you have to dig the hard ground, soften the ground and plant the seed. The hard ground may be the hardness of your heart which has been hardened by doubt and unbelief of God's word for you (Matt. 13:18, 19). The seed needs to be watered and the area around it must not become infected with weeds that would choke out the Word by having its positive effect. When the seed is cared for long enough, it starts to take root and grows. This reminds us that we need to be patient because the roots and the plant itself are not evident until after the initial stages of planting have taken place. It's the same principle in the spiritual context. When we read God's word, we need to plant the goodness of His word in our heart by believing and confessing His word for us. We continue to water His word by meditating and confessing His word. When we do it long enough, we develop a root of having strong faith and the assurance of His word. We then can see the harvest coming about. This harvest can be compared to receiving a physical healing, financial healing, deliverance from different bondages including habitual sins and other needs. We use the goodness of God's pure and holy word to plant and cultivate in our heart so that we may receive the best possible harvest. The weeds that may come up are negative thinking which causes a person to doubt God's word and may result in unbelief (Matt. 13:38b, 39). This is the full context of the parable of the seed and the sower that Jesus explains in Matt. 13:3-9.

By planting God's word in our hearts, we are planting seeds of truth and life, because Jesus is considered the Word (John 1:1, 14) and Jesus tells us He is the Way, Truth and Life (John 14:6). So when we know He is the Way, Truth and Life by His word and our heart is the ground, then we can see the vitality of planting His word into our spirit because whatever we believe in our heart, the issues of what we believe spring up in our lives. Proverbs 4:20-23 gives a perfect illustration regarding His word and the importance of planting His word in our hearts. Listening and inviting any words that oppose what God says about you and for you will eventually allow a person to be deceived and believe the lies of the enemy who is out to steal, kill and eventually destroy you (John 10:10a). That is why, when a person hangs around certain people long enough, they think and become who they hang around with. When someone is negative and blasphemous, we become like them when we are around those types of people long enough. That is why the truth of His word reveals that, "Bad company corrupts good character" (1 Cor. 15:33). In addition, 2 Tim. 3:8, 9 indicates how people's words can have a detrimental effect if we are not careful to weed those out of our lives. When we expect to reap a good harvest, we need to plant His word in our heart, by believing what He says. We need to keep it watered and remove any weeds of doubt by not accepting the subtle lies of the enemy whenever it opposes the encouragement of what God's word says.

Also, if we expect to receive peace and loving kindness from others, we will first have to learn how to plant the very same seeds by our actions towards each other. When we are merciful to one another, we will receive mercy from the One whom we desperately need it from to begin with, which is God. Blessed are the merciful, for they shall receive mercy (Matt. 5:7). When we fail to show mercy to one another, we forget that God often showed mercy to us, when we were never deserving of it otherwise. God's mercy keeps us from receiving what we truly deserve, His punishment, which He has ultimately pardoned us from. His grace we often receive as His blessings which we do not deserve. Oftentimes, we may not feel like showing mercy to others, especially when we have been rejected, wrongfully accused, or have received injustice. The problem is when we fail to show mercy, even to our enemies, we are the only ones who really suffer the consequences by harboring bitterness. It eats away at us which sooner or later will destroy us. We suffer the consequences of losing our joy and peace within us which nothing in this world could ever satisfy. We do ourselves the most injustice by following our fickle feelings and emotions rather than seeing God's precious truth about following His advice which brings healing, liberty, and peace of mind. One of the sermons I heard this past week gave excellent advice, whereby, we need to be determined as God's children to be a blessing to others and make up our minds first and foremost that we have forgiven those who not only have come against us, but will also come against us. This way, when we make up our minds to do what God says to do, we are establishing a hedge of protection around us that violates what the enemy himself has set out to do against us in the first place. We replace negative thinking in our lives, which would destroy us by harboring bitterness, envy, jealousy, and when we replace it by our right thinking of how we can make a positive difference in people's lives, we will benefit by being filled with His peace, joy and health. This is what it means to live an abundant life.

We have to focus on who the real enemy is in the first place (the devil and his angels) and the only way we can effectively defeat our enemy is to do exactly what God tells us to do. When we pray for our enemies, we are praying for those who do not know any better and have been blinded by the real enemy himself, the devil. When we choose not to forgive others, do we really cause our offenders to be justified? What good does it do them when we don't forgive? Do you think for a moment they will be adversely affected? The only one who really hurts when people do not forgive is themselves and no one else. So why do yourself more injustice, because you are simply playing into the tricks of the devil himself.

When you realize that God's word is His cry to you to bless you the most and the only way to liberate you with His awesome peace, joy, and gladness, you will desire His way for you because this is the only remedy that works best for you. Jesus mentions about giving us the oil of joy instead of mourning, and the garments of praise instead of heaviness (Isaiah. 61:3). Many people are sick and in the hospital because they suffer from the injustices which they have never allowed God's word of instruction to heal them. Jesus talks about people who harbor envy within, and the results are like rottenness to the bones (Proverbs 14:30). This is what destroys many people's health, and the devil is fulfilling his purpose by robbing people from living in divine health (3 John 2). He is killing people through a slow and painful death and ultimately destroys people's lives.

The process to overcome his ways is to confess your need to God and acknowledge His divine help for you and receive His word with gladness of heart, knowing that this is His remedy for you to live the abundant life which He longs to give you. When you realize the ultimate sacrifice He lived during His life, he suffered greatly and died the shameful death on the cross for you personally. You will most benefit from His divine word of life that will have a greater impact, just like His wisdom and unsearchable knowledge that continues to call out to you (Proverbs 8:1-12). God will never allow humans to give an account because of their lack of intellect, but He will have each one give an account when we lack the knowledge of His word, by rejecting His instructions. Jesus says that, "My people are destroyed from of lack of knowledge, because you have rejected knowledge" (Hosea 4:6a). We need to allow this mindset to travel from our heads and into our hearts. In other words, when we meditate continually, we will receive that revelation knowledge that gets into our spirit, knowing without a shadow of any doubt that God loves us and yearns to give us what is ultimately best for us. We will please Him the most by obeying His instructions, because we know it is the best remedy for us to live the blessed life here in the present life and in the expanse of the eternal realm. So when God mentions to pray for your enemies and do good to those who persecute you, if you do these things, you yourself will be blessed. By doing this, you ultimately benefit mostly by not allowing the shackles of bitterness, envy and anger to keep you in bondage to the real enemy. In the amplified version of the Bible, when it talks about people being blessed, they are the ones who are envied by those who are not blessed, because the people who reject God choose to do things their way and will never be blessed because of it. We do ourselves more injustice when we choose to do things our way and when we "think" our ways are better than "His" ways. We are most effective and will have victory over defeat, when we make a confession and determine in our hearts to love God by obeying His loving and perfect ways and purposely proceed by moving forward to be doers of His word. Therefore, when we want to reap the very best for ourselves, we first need to sow the proper seeds by allowing God to take control of us by His spirit and we must desire His perfect will for ourselves. We need to confess this to God. It's important we confess, because in comparison to our salvation, it's not just by believing that we are saved, but it is by our confession of our belief that we are saved when we accepted Jesus as our Lord and savior (Rom. 10:10).

When you understand how much He loves you and cares for you; you will love the instructions of His word, which is the very key to reaping the abundant life He longingly wants to give you. It will allow you not to be robbed by the one who equally wants to destroy you. God gives you a choice, to either choose life or death. God wants people to open their hearts and receive life that He suffered greatly in order to give us.

SECTION IV

Blessings To Be Children Of The Light

Chapter 21

WORSHIPPING THE LORD

I sense a heaviness in my spirit that many evangelical churches that profess Christianity lack a real sense and have lost the truth of the real meaning of *worship*. I truly believe that the true sense of the meaning of *worship* lacks the power that is meant to be and we use this term very loosely. As an example, many will use this term just to mean going to a church service. The perception of the term *worship* has lost its impact in what I believe it is meant to be. Many people say that they will go to a worship service, in which all they do is sing a couple of songs, hear a couple of announcements, say or read a couple verses of prayers and listen to a sermon. That is nothing close to worship in the context I believe God indicates in His word and how the people in Biblical times came before God with hungry hearts. Real worship is a lifestyle we live each day as His true followers who are hungry to have a deeper relationship with God. I desire and pray more than ever to see Christians hunger for more of God, to reverence Him, know Him in the beauty of holiness and get on our knees before Him, lifting up holy hands in adoration to Him. I pray that many Christians will get fed up with lukewarm, half-baked so called "mediocre worship" (Read Rev. 3:15-16) and come before Him in reverence by bowing humbly before Him, lifting up holy hands, clapping hands and shouting cries of joy unto Him as it says in Psalm 47. If there are Christians opposed to this, they should read their Bibles more closely and read what God has to say about clapping hands and making a joyful noise unto Him! Many psalms including Psalm 138:1, 2 reveal David's heart and how he longed to praise Him and reverently bow before Him. It's almost embarrassing that the Moslems come as they do and bow before their god, and we barely see ourselves doing that before the true living and holy God who is the only one who is worthy of such honor. How much more should we bow before our God (who is above all) in adoration? Job 40, and 41 and Psalm 139 are a couple of chapters I enjoy reading about the awesome and sovereign glory and power of our Lord. When I meditate on those chapters and consider His sovereign power, and His awesome love for us, it moves me to reverence Him in adoration when I meditate on His awesome attributes. I'm also at fault for lacking to give God genuine praise and worship. I use myself as an example, that if I spent half as much time praising and worshipping God as I do praying for my "needs," I would be much better off and I'd be much more blessed with the power of His anointing. I truly believe that King David was considered a man after God's own heart because of his longing to praise, adore and worship Him. Although he sinned greatly, this is one of the indications that God desires to forgive us of our sins when we repent. However, David was favored by God because he became passionate and coveted a deep relationship with God. I pray that the word, "worship" will have the full and genuine impact it is meant to have in our hearts and the way we live in adoration towards Him on a daily basis. Just like Peter did, when he walked by, the people felt the power of God as his shadow passed by them (Acts 5:15). I pray that we would hunger to worship Him, fear Him, praise Him and love Him like we never have seen or experienced before. I pray that God would impart this desire for all who read this and be so blessed to come into the Holy of Holies, lifting up holy hands, bowing before Him in reverence and hungry to see more power and then His Spirit can move like we often read in the Biblical times; especially in Acts when the presence and the power of God's Holy Spirit was present before thousands and saved many (Acts 2:41). God is not just seeking anyone, but Jesus says, "The Father is seeking worshippers who will worship Him in spirit and in truth. God is Spirit, and His worshippers must worship Him in spirit and in truth" (John 4:23,24). We need to ask God to put within us the burning desire to reverence Him and worship Him like never before, as we empty ourselves and long for His awesome presence in our midst. After all, this is the real purpose why man was created in the first place, so we may worship Him (Isa. 43:7). God tells us to be still and know that I am God (Psalm 46:10), to meditate silently on His awesome power, knowledge, wisdom and His love for you. Let us be the ones whom the Father seeks as we worship Him in spirit and in truth, in the beauty of holiness (Psalm 29:2 and Psalm 96:9).

Chapter 22

Attributes Of God—Part I

When I often think about eternity and realize it in a most profound way, I realize more and more that this life on earth is so temporal that it is a place we need to strive to do our utmost to prepare for our real home that awaits us in the eternal realm.

I compared a little droplet of water, representing my present life here on earth, to the vast enormous oceans of this world representing eternity. If you imagine the Pacific ocean alone, that is over sixty-nine million square miles, eleven-thousand miles across the equator, eight-thousand miles north/south and in several places, the ocean reaches seven miles deep. It's mind-boggling to comprehend eternity in that realm and beyond, because there is no end to eternity! That little drop of water can be compared to a whole life of a person who has lived for one-hundred years. Can you imagine when someone dies at that age without Christ, having worked all those years, labored, accumulated possessions, and strived for recognition, etc? It's like that little drop of water that soon vanishes. Without Christ, that person steps into that vast and enormous realm of eternity with no hope in sight. There is nothing more devastating than knowing that! No wonder in Ecclesiastes, that Solomon, who was considered one of the wisest men to ever live, would say that all is vanity, unless you have confessed to Jesus, for Him to be your personal Lord and savior and acknowledge Him in your life. In the end, nothing else is going to matter. It makes me realize more than ever, that our present lives here and now are simply a preparation of where our eternal home will be. We will all live in an eternal realm. However, the choice is ours to make right now where we will spend eternity, by either allowing Him to sit on the throne of our hearts and receive

Him to be our Lord and Saviour (Rom 10:9,10) or reject Him by not accepting His word and offer of salvation! That is where we will continue to exist in a realm without end. The realm of eternity is beyond any human's understanding or comprehension. No wonder the Lord encourages and admonishes us to set our affections on things above, and not on the things of this world (Col. 3: 2). The Bible is His hearts cry for you to come to Him because He knows the eternal devastation of people rejecting Him.

I also like to compare that drop of water to the world's oceans similarly in every aspect, like comparing my finite (extremely limited) love to His infinite (unlimited) love. With this in mind, I know whatever happens to me, I can have peace knowing that He loves me unconditionally and truly cares for me (Eph. 3:18). In the same way, I compare my insignificant knowledge to the richness of His knowledge (Psalm 139:17, 18 and Isaiah 55:9). Think for a moment when you consider what Christ says in (Matt. 12:36), that every idle word that every human speaks will have to give an account before God. With over six billion inhabitants in this world, the average man speaks about 8,000 words a day while the women speak about an average of 25,000 words a day. This is not mentioned to say anything against women. However, if we take into consideration that many children and mute people can't speak, we will narrow the average to about 10,000 words each person speaks in this world each day. That is like totaling over sixty-trillion words spoken each day. In comparison, sixty-trillion is like counting two thousand times for each second for a hundred years without stopping. Yet God Himself knows every word spoken each day at that astronomical number. This doesn't even take into consideration the thoughts and motives of man. I don't know about you, but it is mind-boggling for me to comprehend such magnitude, that His knowledge is too great for me to fathom, just like David exclaims in (Psalm 139:6).

When I think of this, I have full confidence to obey and trust Him. I know I'm receiving the very best advice to live the most blessed life when I start to understand His awesome knowledge. I like to use the same illustration to compare my wisdom to His infinite wisdom. With this in mind, I have peace and confidence knowing that He is able to mold me and fashion me as a vessel of honor because He knows BEST! When I compare my limited skills and ability to His awesome strength and power, I'm at peace knowing that there is no problem too great that He can't handle for me, no matter what situation I may be going through. He is able to provide, preserve and protect me when I commit any situation in His hands. When we put our hope or trust in man, our work, money, the economy, government, or anything created rather than on God himself, it is like having this drop of water which soon vanishes and represents a hopeless end rather than having the endless hope of joy, peace, gladness, and prosperity, by trusting in Him and having that eternal hope of glory. When I have my mind, heart, and affections set upon His awesomeness and greatness, He enables me to:

1. Be freed from the bondages by not harboring bitterness or un-forgiveness from the past;
2. Be able to pray for my enemies;
3. Not become critical or judgmental towards others, but prayerful;
4. No longer worry about being a people pleaser, or what others may think or say of me;
5. Not being competitive with one another (i.e., at school or work);
6. Be completely content with little, and we can then truly say, "The Lord is my Shepherd, there is nothing I shall be in want of;"
7. Never be envious of others, no matter what;
8. Never be disappointed because I didn't get recognized or awarded for my "good deeds" or accomplishments; and
9. He helps me to resist and have victory over sin and temptation.

By setting my heart, mind, and affections on the hope of His love, greatness, and our eternal glory, it liberates me from the bondages I just mentioned as a result, rather than putting my hope and trust in this world. Where the world will fail sooner or later, God NEVER fails. When I think of this awesome realm of eternity, the trials I live through in this life may seem like a great mountain to most, but they become like a little pebble because our God is awesome, and we can say to this mountain, "Be ye cast into the depths of the sea and does not doubt in his heart but believes that what he says will happen, it will be done for him." (Mark 11:23). God has really been impressing my heart in a way in which I have such a deeper and more complete fellowship and relationship with Him. I do have hope that as you meditate on this, it will most encourage you as it has for me. And with hope, I can exclaim the promise of this scripture, "For I consider that our present sufferings are not worth comparing with the glory that will be revealed in us" (Rom. 8:18).

Chapter 23

ATTRIBUTES OF GOD—PART II

There is no place in the universe that God was not present everywhere at any given moment in time. There was never a moment in history that God didn't know all things. His knowledge is so great that He foreknew every event and every human life before the foundation of the world (Eph. 1:4; Rom. 8:29, 30). There are even some Christians that don't believe in the fore-knowledge of God, which is very sad to say. In Jeremiah 1:5, God tells us that before I formed you in the womb I knew you. If Christians don't believe in the fore-knowledge of God, how can they explain the prophecies explained in the old testament which Christ Himself fulfilled many years later. How was it that Jesus knew who was going to betray Him for 30 pieces of silver before it ever happened? Also, how was it that He knew Peter was going to deny Him three times before the rooster crowed twice (Mark 14:30)? These people may as well rip out the pages in Revelation from chapter 4 right through to the end of chapter 22 because these are events that are yet to come, with which Christ Himself has predicted in His foreknowledge! His almighty power is also beyond comparison. If all the world and the powers and principalities were to fight against the Lord, the Lord would prevail in every circumstance. For it is not man's plans that succeed him, but it is God who directs his steps (Proverbs 16:9). Many people will oppose this theory, but the problem is not with God, but the fact that we have failed to understand His awesome ways and have treaded on thin ice by having limited Him to our limited comprehension of Him. If we could figure out God or comprehend Him in any way, then He would not be God, nor would He be worthy of our worship. It's vitally important that we do not limit Him in any way, but acknowledge Him far greater than we can ever comprehend. As I mentioned earlier, sadly, many Christians have limited the power, knowledge, and wisdom of our God. I believe they are treading on very thin ice when they do so. The reason Jesus could not perform the miracles of God is because of unbelief (Matt. 13:58). When I ponder the sovereignty of His greatness, I learn to develop reverential fear for Him. This is not just an imaginative theory, but it is a vital truth to know about God. There is a real danger of ever limiting God in our minds. Like I mentioned before, if we could always figure out God, and limit Him in any way to our own understanding, He would not be God. He would not be worthy of our worship. That is why He has every right to be a jealous God. God indicates His indignation towards His people when they lost their awe of Him (Jer. 2:19).

When I meditate upon His awesome glory, power, infinite wisdom and knowledge (Psalm 139:1-6), I'm no longer being robbed of the fullness of joy, peace, and gladness that only He is able to offer me. We never have to rely on a "favorable situation" to have His joy and peace within us. Because Paul and Silas knew God so intimately, even the prison cells could not stop them from singing praises unto Him. They knew who they were in Christ, and knew Him as an awesome creator! Trials, afflictions, and unfavorable conditions which may seem like Mount Everest will seem like a little pebble when we keep our heart set upon His eternal glory. As it has helped me overcome a lot of bondages, it has also helped me to become more Christ-like. When I meditate on His great attributes and read His word as His love letter to me, it makes me want to:

- Be "My utmost for His Highest;"
- Be the arms to embrace those who are hurting;
- Be the hands to hold those who need encouragement;
- Be the soft shoulder for those who need to shed tears on;
- Be the feet to walk the extra mile with those who are trodding through the valley of discouragement; and
- To bless the lonely and the sick with the best gift of all—my time.

I'm most encouraged to do this when I keep my eyes on Him and my hope is in eternity in His glorious kingdom, helping those in need without any selfish ambition or worldly gain. It will allow us to want to be as a humble child and with this hope, we will be among the greatest in the Kingdom of God (Matt. 18:1-4). We inherit the richness of His reward for all eternity without end. Remember, He is always willing and able to do more than what we ever ask or can imagine (Eph. 3:20).

I've been most encouraged by continually meditating on these thoughts, because if I had kept my eyes upon my present circumstances and hopes of ever making it through this life alone, I would be most miserable and discouraged like I have experienced many times in the past. But by His grace and mercy, He has impressed upon my heart to set my hopes and affections on Jesus and the hope of eternal glory He alone is able and willing to offer. Just as eternity itself is beyond our imagination, so is our awesome God who made it all possible.

Chapter 24

Who Will Be the Greatest in His Kingdom?

When we see our focus for our destiny, would it not make sense that it's best not only to make it into heaven, but to become among the greatest in the kingdom of God? I believe in the greater and lesser eternal rewards, just like I believe in the greater and lesser condemnation that Jesus spoke to the Pharisees about. Jesus describes the greater rewards to those in leadership positions who do His will, and He talks about those who have that childlike faith receiving greater rewards. Also, it was the Pharisees, Sadducees and teachers of the law which Jesus often warned that they would bear the greater condemnation because of their pompous, so-called self-righteous attitude. In 1 Cor. 3:10-15, it plainly says that though many will enter into heaven, they will do so by narrowly escaping through the flames. I don't know about you, but I don't want to be one of those who get into heaven just by narrowly escaping flames of fire! God says each of us will be tried by fire, and there are going to be a lot of people whose "works" will be tried and burned up whereby they will have little or no rewards at all. If this is so, then we have failed in our love for God, in our submission to Him, and His authority, we didn't seek Him as much as we should have. When we look deeper into the fiery trials being tried, that's when we have gone through adversity and the result of our reward depends on how we deal with the situation. In other words, if someone or several people come against you, accuse you, mock you, and you retaliate against them, you would not be acting any different than how the world would react. If this is so, this is what is described as our "works" being burned up as wood, hay, and stubble which results in no reward. When we react to adversity like Jesus instructs us to, and we pray for our enemies like He tells us to, give our enemy a drink when he is thirsty, and hold no grudge against them, this is when we are tried. We will be adorned like precious jewels that became that way because they went through the fire also. We are guaranteed wonderful and great rewards when we are proven through trials and obey the Lord. Therefore, we need to consider adversity as an opportunity to be richly rewarded rather than fret over this momentary trouble in time (Read Rom. 8:18).

In Matt. 18:1-4, the disciples asked Jesus, "Who will be the greatest in the kingdom of Heaven?" Jesus answered, "Do you see this young child? You will by no means enter the kingdom of God unless you become as this child. Therefore, whoever humbles himself like this child is the greatest in the kingdom of heaven." In essence, if we become among the greatest in heaven, would it not mean that God is most pleased with us? Should that not be our ultimate goal? Eternity is an awesome realm in itself and it's sad for the people who are not only eternally lost, but enter into heaven, having perhaps very little rewards and losing the greater rewards they could have received in the realm for all eternity. Therefore, it is safe to say we will have pleased the Father most when we humble ourselves like a child as He said in His word. Notice when you think of a child that the heavenly Father is most pleased with a child who doesn't have a PhD, a doctorate degree, a decoration or is able to debate a matter. A child who loves will never question his father's authority, his integrity, and his instruction. Rather, he will always honor him, trust him, and obey, regardless of how it may seem because he loves him and the child knows his father loves him and truly believes his father will care and provide for him. When you think that a child should be so blessed by having this kind of relationship with his earthly father, don't you think we should have this kind of loving relationship with our heavenly Father that much more?

When we become humble like a child, we, too, can become among the greatest in the kingdom of God. When we have great rewards in His kingdom, we will undoubtedly know He is most pleased with us. I pray that we would remain humble under His authority and one with another, and receiving and embracing the rich treasures of

His word throughout our whole being. For His divine instruction of His word to have its greatest impact on us, we need to embrace His word, by having a childlike faith, attitude, and be adults in our thinking. Having true childlike faith is having a right heart when we desire to be His followers. We must embrace Him as our loving Lord as He sits in authority in the throne of our heart. May this bless you and I pray that you will ask and accept God's help and guidance, to be a child who loves His heavenly Father. He promises to richly reward you now and for all eternity when you do so.

Chapter 25

RECEIVING HIS GLORIOUS AND ETERNAL REWARDS

Many Christians today become discouraged and remain in bondage when they desire to be recognized or rewarded for their efforts. God may be telling you not to be weary for doing good, because great will be our reward if we do not give up (read Gal 6:9). He encourages us not to be discouraged when we feel we deserve an award or recognition of some sort and we don't get it. Have you ever been discouraged because you didn't get recognized, or someone else took the credit you deserved instead? For many years, I've sought to get recognition for my efforts and be rewarded openly for them. I also received many disappointments because I didn't receive the honor from people I felt I deserved. I was under bondage of pleasing people and being recognized by people rather than pleasing God. It was a real bondage because putting your trust in people will cause you to be frustrated because they will sooner or later fail you. A most prestigious award that anyone could ever receive, even in front of cameras or the limelight is a glory to be received for a mere moment in time, like a small breath in a massive hurricane. If we get caught up trying to outdo one another just to receive a moment's glory, we have utterly failed to receive glory from the One who is able to give and be rewarded for all eternity. What a tragedy that will be when many people will expect to be rewarded by God and they won't receive it, all because they sought to be rewarded by man, and they chose to deny the rewards that come from God which will last forever. Many people will lose their rewards forever just because they chose to have a moment's glory here on earth. I would dare say that any reward from God far exceeds any reward man could ever present to anyone. When we labor out of love for God, our reward is so great that it is everlasting in all eternity. Again, if we seek to receive an award or be rewarded by man for doing good works, we have been robbed of receiving His reward for doing the same thing for all eternity. Jesus says to the teachers of the law, "If you receive the praises of men, what reward do you receive from my Father, because you have received your reward already?" (Matt. 6:5,6.) I imagine this would have been devastating news when they realized they had failed to receive the rewards that would last forever simply because they sought the favor and praises of man. Know that we will be rewarded for being in our prayer closets where no one else knows but God Himself who sees all things. Jesus says that even if you give a cup of cold water in my name, and not seek recognition, your reward will be great in heaven (Matt. 10:42). I'd rather receive God's reward for all eternity simply by offering a cold cup of water in His name without being noticed than receiving a distinguished Order of Merit medal from our governor general, or any worldly acclaimed award such as the Nobel peace prize. It's like a verse in a song we sing, that I'd rather be faithful to His dear holy name than to receive men's applause, glory and fame.

The rewards received from God alone will be forever; never be destroyed by moth, rust nor ever be stolen (Matt. 6:19-21). You do not need to have a great ministry like Billy Graham to be richly rewarded by the heavenly Father. As long as you are faithful and believe in Him (John 6:28, 29), He is most pleased with you. I have seen many people in my old workplace not be faithful and they got promoted instead of me. However, as I see it now, it was a blessing for me not to be rewarded because I would not have had the privilege of attaining several positions I presently enjoy the most, had I gotten promoted. Through it all, I have been blessed in far greater ways that no one can compare who are living outside of the will of God.

There is a hidden blessing when we cannot see it for ourselves right away, because God will always make a way for us when we put our trust in Him. When we think otherwise, we are really telling God that we doubt that He is fair and just. We serve a God who is absolute and perfectly just and faithful. He is able to do exceedingly to those who love the Lord. It's a liberation that I look forward to each day to do the best I can as God's representative at work. I have no selfish desire or seek to receive any glory or recognition, but rather, I look forward to the day where God will reward us greatly, and that will last for all eternity instead. It's one thing to be recognized for your good works as you desire to please the Lord, than to simply to be ambitious only to receive man's recognition. This is why Jesus admonishes us to set our affections on things above, and not on things (or ambitions) of this world (Col. 3:2). He wants our affections to reflect on eternal values in comparison to its eternal rewards other than temporal values and its lesser rewards. He desires that we receive the greater rewards because of His great love for us. He is always willing that we would not suffer loss because of our selfish ways.

I encourage you to pray that you will not be caught up in bondage to labor just to be awarded by man, or just to receive their recognition for only a moment's glory. But, you would labor as unto the Lord out of love for Him in obedience and be highly rewarded, receiving that incorruptible crown of glory that lasts FOREVER (1 Cor. 9:24, 25).

Printed in the United States
135056LV00001B/16/P